HOW TO DO YOUR OWN ADVERTISING

In this Series

Other titles in preparation

DO YOUR OWN
ADVERTISING

The secrets of successful sales promotion

Michael Bennie

Second edition

How To Books

Cartoons by Mike Flanagan

British Library Cataloguing in Publication Data
A catalogue record for this book is available from the British Library.

Published by How To Books Ltd, Plymbridge House, Estover Road,
Plymouth PL6 7PZ, United Kingdom. Tel: (01752) 735251/695745.
Fax: (01752) 695699. Telex: 45635.

First edition 1990
Second edition (revised) 1996

Note: The material contained in this book is set out in good faith for general
guidance and no liability can be accepted for loss or expense incurred as a
result of relying in particular circumstances on statements made in the book.
The law and regulations may be complex and liable to change, and readers
should check the current position with the relevant authorities before making
personal arrangements.

Produced for How To Books by Deer Park Productions.
Typeset by PDQ Typesetting, Stoke-on-Trent, Staffs.
Printed and bound by The Cromwell Press, Broughton Gifford, Melksham,
Wiltshire.

Contents

List of Illustrations

Acknowledgements

I would like to acknowledge with thanks the kind permission of the following to use their advertisements in this book:

BRAD
The Fashion House
Bourne Sports Ltd
Town and Country Driveways Ltd
Swiss Bank Corporation
ESPA Pumps (UK) Ltd
Birkbeck College, University of London
Brookes & Gatehouse Ltd
Regent Products
MM Advertising & Public Relations
David & Charles Publishers plc

My thanks also go to Mike Lyons for checking chapters 5 and 8 for me, and for his useful suggestions and the tactful way in which he made them.

IS THIS YOU?

Retailer	Hotelier	Publican
Charity organiser	Financial consultant	Manufacturer
Fundraiser	Freelance worker	Accountant
Solicitor	Builder	Entrepreneur
Travel agent	Insurance broker	Plumber
Management consultant	Electrician	Event organiser
Chiropractor	Marketing manager	Head teacher
Osteopath	Theatre manager	Interior designer
Club secretary	Acupuncturist	Homeopath
Campsite proprietor	Tour operator	Computer consultant
Leisure centre manager	Garage proprietor	Hire company owner
Landscape designer	Central heating engineer	Craftsman
Cleaning consultant	Shopfitter	Restaurateur
College principal	Optician	Caterer
Mortgage broker	Aromatherapist	Engineering consultant
Tourist attraction owner	Hairdresser	Glazier
Coach operator	Antique dealer	Photographer

Preface
to the second edition

This book is for anyone who needs – or wants – to advertise effectively, but who does not want to pay agency rates. I hope it will also be useful to those who simply want to know what is involved in advertising, whether as students, business people or interested laymen.

Whether you are a retailer or a manufacturer, a service industry or a voluntary organisation, it is likely that at some stage you will need to advertise a product, a service or an event, and most of you will need to do so regularly. How do you ensure that you get the most from your advertising; that *yours* is the product that gets seen – and bought?

Anyone can put together a mediocre ad, and they will probably get at least some response. With proper planning and the right techniques, however, you can make your ad very much more effective and eye-catching and increase that response by 300 per cent and more – sometimes without even spending any more money.

There is no great secret about composing effective ads – even the design can be done by someone with a little imagination and creativity. Of course, if you want to compete with some of the classic ads you see on television and in the national press, then an agency (and a very deep pocket) is essential. There is no way an amateur can compete in that sort of league. But few if any small business people actually need to advertise in that way; there is no reason why you should not put together a simple, straightforward, yet effective ad or brochure with the minimum of outside help.

This book is written in the order in which you should be working – from choosing the right media, through the brief, the design, the copywriting, to analysing the results of your campaign. I have tried to explain every step clearly, with the lay reader in mind. There are illustrations, examples of actual ads, case studies to show the principles in practice, and questionnaires and checklists to help you check your progress. For those who want to become more involved, there are suggestions for further reading, and a list of useful addresses. The aim throughout is to make advertising easy and enjoyable; after all, if *you* are not enthusiastic about it, it is going to be difficult to make your readers enthusiastic!

Much has changed in the world of advertising since the first edition of this book, and this new edition takes account of those changes. One of the most important, in terms of practical techniques, has been the explosion in the use of information technology. Professional designers now all use computerised systems, and many amateurs also have them. But do not be deceived into thinking that a desktop publishing system, no matter how sophisticated, will in itself improve your design skills, and that if you possess such a system you can skip chapters 5 and 8. It may make the design process less laborious, but you still need to know how to create a good design, and many of the procedures are similar whether you are working on a DTP system or by hand.

Throughout, the book refers to whatever it is that you are advertising as your 'product', although many of you will be advertising a service or an event rather than a product as such. This is purely for convenience; most techniques apply equally to anything you may be advertising. Where prices are quoted in the case studies, these are only rough examples. They should not be taken as an indication of the actual costs involved.

We will cover most kinds of printed advertising, from small classified ads to colourful brochures, but not radio and television. These require very different techniques, and you should consult your local TV or radio station for advice on those media.

Doing your own advertising does not mean you have to have all the requisite skills yourself. You can employ freelance workers for certain jobs and do others yourself. It all depends on your particular aptitudes and preferences. What is important, however, is to give yourself enough time to do the job properly. A good ad cannot be produced in a hurry at the last minute: every stage needs careful thought, especially if it is your first attempt.

Finally, don't give up if you don't get it absolutely right. Even the professionals don't produce perfect ads every time. We have all seen ads and thought, 'If only they hadn't used that colour combination' or, 'What on earth made them choose that headline?' Although they might not admit it, you would probably find that the designer and copywriter concerned were saying the same to themselves! The secret is to learn from each ad and campaign. Analyse them, check the media, measure the response, and tailor future efforts accordingly.

Michael Bennie

1
Why Advertise?

Advertising is an essential part of almost any marketing plan. You may have a product that the public is crying out for, something for which there is a genuine need. But unless you tell them that it is there, what it can do for them and how to get hold of it, you might just as well not bother to produce it. This may seem self-evident, but it is surprising how many people believe that a good product will 'sell itself'. Whether your ads are simple or sophisticated, whether you use several media or just one or two, will depend on your product and your market. But there are very few businesses which can reach their full potential without any advertising at all.

REASONS FOR ADVERTISING

There are many reasons for advertising. Some of the most important are to:

- announce a new product or a modification to an old one

- reach new buyers

- announce a sale or special offer

- invite enquiries

- invite sales

- maintain sales

- keep ahead of the competition.

Most businesses advertise for a combination of reasons, and perhaps with a combination of different types of ad. For example, if you only advertise sales or special offers, you could distort your image: the public are likely to associate you with special offers, rather than with the quality you offer during the rest of the year.

A retailer with a high street site may feel that he or she can get all the business needed from passing trade. Why spend money on advertising, they may say, when people can see the shop for themselves whenever they go to town? And of course, high street shops *do* get a lot of passing trade. But there is probably *more* business to be had with effective advertising. What about attracting shoppers from outside the area? Or those who do most of their shopping at out-of-town hypermarkets? Perhaps there is another shop down the street, selling the same range of goods. Or perhaps someone else sets up in competition who does advertise, and starts drawing your trade away.

- If you are in business, you have something to sell, even if it is your own services. If you do not advertise, you will not fulfil your sales potential.

TYPES OF ADVERTISEMENT

There are a number of ways in which you can advertise, and they fall into five main categories:

- press advertising

- direct response advertising

- brochures

- sales letters

- posters.

Press advertising

As its name implies, **press advertising** is advertising which appears in a newspaper or magazine. It includes **direct response ads** and **inserts**, which will be dealt with later, as well as **display** and **classified** advertisments. Classified ads are usually grouped together, and classified under headings according to what is being advertised. Many classified ads now have a 'display' element, and some even include pictures. Display ads can appear in any part of the newspaper or magazine; they are usually designed, and the advertiser can have some say in where or how they appear.

Pros
- It can be used in some form for just about any kind of product or service.

Cons
- It can sometimes reach *too* wide an audience. You could end up paying for a circulation of 100,000, of whom only half are really potential customers for what you have to offer.

- Unless you use inserts, you are restricted in your layout.

- It can be difficult to measure the response, unless you use direct response advertising.

Direct response advertising
Press ads which include a **coupon** or invite customers to send in for the product, or for information on it, are called **direct response** ads. Although you can just invite people to write in for the product, it is best to include a cut-out coupon in the ad. That way, you ensure that customers provide all the information you need to process their orders.

Pros
- As with other press ads, you can take as much or as little space as you need to get your message across.

- As with other press ads, you can reach a large number of people.

- If you code the coupon in some way, you can see exactly where each order came from, and measure the success of each ad. For example if advertising in *Exchange & Mart* for the first time, you could tell customers to reply to 'Dept EM1' of your business.

Cons
- You are still restricted in your layout, as you are with other ads.

- You could still be paying to reach too wide an audience.

- There are certain requirements to be met, especially if you ask for payment in advance (see p. 30).

- Readers may be reluctant to 'deface' a magazine or newspaper by cutting out coupons.

- If you send goods on approval rather than asking for payment in advance, you will almost certainly face some non-payment.

Direct response advertising is useful if you are selling goods direct to the public. It cannot be used, however, where there is no product that you can send to the customer – ie if you offer a service, if your product is distributed through the retail trade, or if you are advertising a shop rather than a particular product.

Brochures

A **brochure** can be just a one-sheet leaflet or a 32-page catalogue. It can be printed in black and white or in full colour. It can be mailed, distributed by hand, or inserted in a magazine. In fact it is probably the most versatile form of advertising available.

Pros
- You have no restrictions on space, which is useful if you have a lot to say.

- If you are distributing it by hand or by post, it is possible to target your market more precisely and avoid waste.

Cons
- If you want to reach a very wide audience, it can be an expensive way of doing it.

- It can be uneconomic if you don't need a lot of space to describe and illustrate your product.

- If it is used as an insert in a magazine, you have no control over where it appears. With an ordinary press ad, you can ask for it to appear in a particular position, opposite certain editorial material, etc.

Sales letters

Despite their name **sales letters** are not letters that your sales force sends out. They are advertisements; they are just as much a part of an advertising campaign as a nicely designed press ad. Think of them as simple brochures. You should certainly put as much time and effort into writing a sales letter as into writing the copy for an ad; it has more in common with an advertisement in terms of style and content than with any other kind of letter. They can be typed, but it is more usual (and gives a better impression) to use a word processor. If typed, they must either be done individually, which takes time, or photocopied, which reduces the quality and thus the impact.

Pros

- They are cheap to produce.

- They can be personalised if you use a word processor.

- They have a more direct impact than most other forms of advertising.

Cons

- They are no use if you need to illustrate your product.

- If you have a large mailing list it can be very time-consuming to personalise each letter. Printed sales letters do not have quite the same impact as a person-to-person communication.

Sales letters are sometimes used by themselves in mailings to consumers, but they are more often used to introduce an accompanying brochure describing the product in more detail. They really come into their own, however, in mailings to a fairly small but well-targeted list of businesses.

Posters

Posters are seen everywhere – in the street, on bus shelters, in railway stations, on buses and the Underground. They can be an effective means of advertising if you can get the right site at the right price.

Pros

- You can pinpoint where people see your ad by choosing a site to suit you – on the road towards your premises, for example, or on the way into town.

- At stations, in bus shelters and on buses, you have a captive audience – very often travellers have nothing to do but read the posters.

Cons

- Outdoor advertising (street sites or the outside of buses) is read 'on the move', and so your message must be short and to the point. In fact, the best outdoor poster advertising usualy consists of a striking illustration and a brief slogan.

- With indoor posters your audience is in one way more specific, but in another way more general than with other media. You are paying to reach everyone who uses the station, or everyone who travels on the bus. This is fine if your target audience is, say, commuters or schoolchildren or housewives going shopping. But if your target audience is the public at large, you will miss a large proportion of them with indoor poster advertising; and if it is a special interest group – say DIY enthiasists – then only a small proportion of the people you are paying to reach will be interested.

CHECKLIST

- Is advertising part of your marketing plan?

- Can your business reach its full potential without advertising?

- Which of the five main methods will suit your business – press ads, direct response ads, brochures, sales letters or posters?

2
What Does Advertising Involve?

A BRIEF GUIDE TO THE PROCESSES

The flowchart in Fig. 1 shows the various stages involved in putting together an ad. Most of them are dealt with in detail in later chapters, but at this stage let us see what these stages are, how they fit together, which functions you can perform yourself, and which you will need expert assistance with.

Media buying
This is the purchase or hire of the *means* of advertising:

- the space for a press ad

- the mailing list for a mailshot

- the site for a poster.

Although there are specialists who offer their services on a commission or fee basis, media buying is something you can easily do yourself.

Layout
Having bought your media, the next stage is to do a **layout** or **visual**. This is an accurate sketch of what the finished ad will look like, but without the actual text or illustration. Examples of layouts are shown in the case studies in chapter 5. Whether or not you do this yourself depends on your own aptitudes and abilities. There is no magic about designing an ad; if you have a certain amount of creativity, there is no reason why you should not do your own layouts.

Copy
Once the layout is done, you can see how much copy and illustration you will need. The **copy** is the text of the ad – the description of the product and its benefits – and writing it is another function which you can perform yourself.

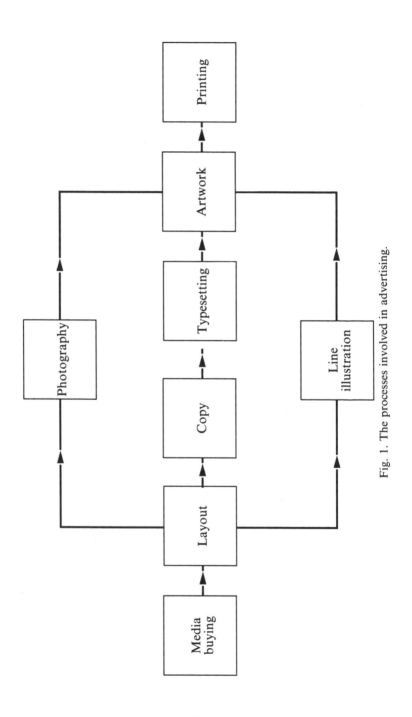

Fig. 1. The processes involved in advertising.

Photography

If you are doing your own photography, on the other hand, you should be competent enough to produce well-composed, high-quality pictures. Because of the way in which photographs are reproduced in print (explained in chapter 8), the average 'holiday-snap' type picture will often be indistinct when reproduced, while poor composition can ruin the effects of an advertising shot.

If you do not have that level of competence, you should hire a professional photographer.

Line illustrations

Similarly, if you have some artistic skill you could make any line drawings (or line and wash illustrations) yourself. Otherwise you will need to employ a professional.

Typesetting

Once you have written the copy, it will need to be **typeset** – each element set in the typeface and size you have chosen, ready to be printed. If you have a sophisticated DTP system you can do this yourself, but most people will need to employ a commercial typesetter; typesetting equipment is complex and very expensive. Alternatively, your printer might be able to offer this service.

Artwork

The **artwork** is the stage at which the two elements – copy and illustration – come together. This is where they are laid down to form the camera-ready 'master', from which your printer makes plates to print the ad. What is required here is precision and an eye for detail. If you used a professional designer at the layout stage, you will no doubt want to use them again for the artwork, but it *is* a job you can do yourself, especially if you have a good DTP system. If you are using colour in your ad, your artwork will need to have an overlay sheet showing what colours are to be used where.

Printing

The next stage is for your artwork to go to the newspaper or magazine in the case of a press ad, or to the printer in the case of a brochure.

HOW MUCH TO SPEND

How to budget for advertising is one of the most vexed questions in business. One textbook outlines seventeen ways in which an advertising budget can be devised!

Some people work on the basis of how much they can afford, which doesn't really help, because 'How much can I afford?' is almost as open-ended as 'How much should I spend?' Others suggest spending a percentage of turnover each year. This helps a little, but not much, because the really difficult part is deciding *what* percentage. The truth is that there is no hard and fast formula for deciding how much to spend on advertising; even if there were, it would need constant modification to allow for different types of business and changing circumstances.

Most businesses spend between one and three per cent of their turnover on advertising, but it can be even less and, in the case of mail order for example, it can be as high as ten or fifteen per cent. Two apparently similar businesses can have very different advertising budgets, both equally valid. To take a simple example, a retailer with a prime high street site might spend less than one per cent of turnover on advertising because large numbers of people pass his door. A competitor in a side street, however, could well need to spend two or three per cent or more, because in a sense, her advertisements will have to be her shop window.

What do you want to achieve?

It is better not to start with the question 'How much should I spend?', but rather 'What do I want to achieve, and how much do I *need* to spend to achieve it?' Then see how this compares with your turnover. The following step-by-step procedure will help you to arrive at a sensible budget.

1. Decide on your precise **objective** in advertising. Is it to launch a new product? To take advantage of a growing market? To increase sales of an existing product? To remind the public that you are there? To maintain sales?

2. Work out what you need to **spend in a year** to achieve this objective. You will probably need to investigate the media as outlined in chapter 3 before you can work this out in any detail.

3. See what this represents as a **percentage** of your anticipated turnover.

4. If it is below one per cent or above three per cent, is there a good reason? Launching a new product, for example, will need more than the average amount of advertising. Direct mail advertising using a colour brochure is likely to be expensive, but may be

necessary. On the other hand, advertising which simply acts as a reminder that you are there may not need such a high budget.

5. If there is no good reason why your budget should be significantly higher or lower than average, perhaps you should go back to stage 2, and see whether you do in fact need to advertise as much as you thought.

The main thing to remember, however, is that no two organisations are the same, and if you are convinced that your budget is right, then the fact that it does not conform to a national average need not bother you.

Plan a cohesive campaign

Plan a full year's advertising, at least in outline, and then 'fine tune' it as you go along. In that way you get some cohesion to your campaign. You can develop a theme, establish your identity and plan your production or sales efforts around the expected responses to your ads. You will focus on priorities and keep the budget under control. If you place ads on an *ad hoc* basis, month by month, things become disjointed, and you won't get the most out of your campaign. You could also miss some of the best advertising times, as there is a temptation to advertise only in those months when you think you can *afford* to do so.

A retail outlet should normally allocate the full year's advertising budget month by month according to each month's sales. If you want to boost business in traditionally 'slow' months, however, you might decide to advertise more in those periods than during busier months. Other businesses will have their own patterns. January is the time when most people plan summer holidays, for example; winter is a good time for plumbers to advertise, because of the possibility of burst pipes; September is good for 'back-to-school' promotions.

Record what you do

When you have your budget, and have spread it over the year, *write it down*. Have a column for each month, and a line for each medium. Pencil in the figures for each; as the results of each ad come in, you can revise your future plans. Don't be too inflexible. If ads in a particular medium fail in January and February, you want to be able to switch to another medium later in the year. You might also want to place an unplanned ad from time to time, to cope with an unforeseen development – a forthcoming price rise, for example, or a particularly cold winter, or the sudden emergence of a competitor.

It is important to keep track of what you *actually* spend, both to check against your budget and to have something against which to measure the response. You can do this by introducing a second column for each month on your budget sheet, but it is probably better to do it separately, so that you can analyse it by ad, and set the response against the cost. A sample ad response analysis is shown on page 162.

The case studies that follow show how the budgeting exercise might work in practice.

CASE STUDIES

Mary advertises her bookshop
Mary Davies runs a bookshop in one of the two main shopping streets of a market town. There is some competition from the branch of a national chain in the other street, but Mary's shop is big enough and well enough established to hold its own.

Because of her position, she gets a lot of passing trade, but she advertises to attract people from the outlying areas served by the town, to draw attention to special 'book-buying' times of year, and to keep the public aware of her shop's existence – an important factor in view of the competition.

She has allocated £1,250 for advertising. This is less than one per cent of her turnover, but she doesn't feel she needs to spend more because her prime site is in itself a form of advertising, and because her bookshop is already well known in the area. Her main advertising months are June for summer reading, September for the winter hobby market and the start of the school year, and December for Christmas. She allocates £340 for each of these three months, with the rest of the budget being spent on monthly 'reminder' ads.

Peter promotes his plumbing business
Peter Jackson is a plumber. He is just setting up on his own, having worked for a contractor for several years, and is taking his younger brother on to help. He needs to get himself established and build up a network of clients, so he is prepared to spend about three per cent of their projected income of £25,000 on advertising. He intends to write to all the local building contractors, offering his services, but that will take very little of his budget. He has considered advertising regularly in his local newspaper, but he takes the view that if someone wants a plumber, they will look in a local directory. He decides, however, to try a few ads in the summer, to see whether he can attract people who are thinking of renewing their central heating. His budget will therefore be allocated as follows:

May	£ 45
June	£ 45
July	£ 45
August	£570
September	£ 45
TOTAL	£750

The video makers

Vidco make instructional video films, and part of their range is a series of three golfing videos. Although they sell a few videos through specialist shops, by far the greatest number of sales comes through direct response advertising in this specialist media.

In trying to achieve the maximum sales, they therefore have to advertise extensively. Since their turnover is directly related to their advertising effort, they are not concerned about what advertising represents as a percentage of turnover. What they need to be sure of, however, is that every ad generates enough sales to justify its existence.

They therefore decide to advertise in the major golfing magazines through the winter. They believe that that is the best time to sell videos, since golfers will want to be out playing throughout the summer, not watching videos. They allow themselves a little leeway, however, to try a few tests, without committing themselves too deeply. They might test one or two of the less popular magazines, and they will probably try one test ad in the summer, to see whether videos *can* be sold in the playing season.

They allocate £11,500 for advertising, and break it down as follows:

October	£1,100
November	£2,100
December	£1,100
January	£1,800
February	£1,800
March	£1,800
June	£1,800

The riding centre

John and Sylvia Talbot have a holiday centre in Wales, offering riding holidays to adults and children. At present they have facilities for twenty people, and they have no trouble filling the centre through a few advertisements in the specialist magazines, and with repeat bookings from satisfied customers. They have just undertaken an extensive building programme, however, which will double the accommodation.

Their objective is therefore to fill the extra places, and they also want to tackle a perennial problem – ensuring as even a spread of business as possible. This means encouraging people to visit them during the off season as well as in the more popular holiday months. They accept that to achieve these objectives they will need, at least initially, to advertise more extensively than they have done in the past. They plan to place small ads in the specialist media, inviting people to send for details of the centre, and to produce a colour brochure to mail to those who respond. They will rent a list of riding enthusiasts to mail to, and will also mail the brochure to their own past customers. In order to attract people out of season, they intend to offer special rates for short breaks, so they will advertise winter breaks in the autumn and summer holidays in January/February. Their budget for this is £12,300.

This figure is high in relation to their projected turnover, but there are two factors which make it acceptable. First, the cost of a colour brochure is high, but it is necessary in order to convey the attractions of the centre and its surrounding countryside; and secondly, they need to advertise more extensively than usual because of the increased accommodation they have to fill.

They divide their budget as follows:

September	Design, photography and printing of brochure	£ 3,750
October	Advertising	£ 1,700
	Mailing list	£ 1,000
November	Advertising	£ 1,700
December	Advertising	£ 100
January	Advertising	£ 1,700
February	Advertising	£ 1,700
Total		£11,650

The cost of postage will be added to that figure, and will be spread over several months, from October to March or April.

LEGAL REQUIREMENTS

The two main laws

There are few laws aimed directly at advertisers, but those concerning trading in general apply equally to advertising. The two trading laws which particularly affect the advertiser are:

● the Sale of Goods Act

● the Trade Descriptions Act.

It is unlikely that you will fall foul of either of these Acts, and you certainly don't need to know them in detail. In essence, they have two main provisions of concern to the advertiser. Goods advertised must be 'fit for the purpose' for which they would normally be used, and they must correspond to your description of them.

You could not, for example, sell a vacuum flask which didn't keep liquids hot, because that is what vacuum flasks are normally used for. Your customer couldn't complain, however, if the flask was damaged when he was using it to keep his screws in. That cannot be classified as normal use!

Probably more important for the advertiser is the requirement that goods must correspond to description. It is, of course, only reasonable that advertisers should describe their products correctly. If your advertisement for the vacuum flask above said that it was useful for keeping screws in, then the customer would have cause for complaint if it was damaged when he used it for that purpose.

Pitfalls to avoid

There are some potential pitfalls, however, particularly in relation to the composition of your product and its price. Just as the label of a product must list its components in descending order, so must an advertisement for it. If you are advertising a dress made of seventy per cent acrylic and thirty per cent wool, you must describe it as being acrylic and wool, not wool and acrylic.

Advertisements are also governed by the same regulations on pricing and price reductions as retail stores; any goods advertised as being reduced must have been offered at the full price for a period of twenty-eight days in the previous six months.

If you contravene the law, or if there is a dispute with a customer over whether you have contravened it or not, it is likely to be referred to the customer's local **Trading Standards Officer**. If he supports the customer, you will be asked to refund any money paid, and to amend your advertisement. As a last resort, you could be prosecuted, but only if you persistently refused to make amends.

Other laws to know about

There are two other laws which might affect some advertisers. If you offer goods on credit terms, the **Consumer Credit Act** requires you to obtain a licence from the Office of Fair Trading. Information can be obtained from your local Trading Standards Department.

If you maintain a mailing list, you could be affected by the **Data**

Protection Act, designed to protect the public against the misuse of personal data held on computer. Even if you just keep a list of names and addresses, you probably need to register with the **Data Protection Registrar** if it is held on computer. The Advertising Association, Abford House, 15 Wilton Road, London SW1V 1NJ (Tel: 0171 828 2771) publish a code of practice on the Act, and will be able to advise you.

THE BRITISH CODE OF ADVERTISING PRACTICE

The **British Code of Advertising Practice** (BCAP) is what is known as a **voluntary code**. Don't be misled by this term. It does *not* mean that you can choose whether to apply it or not! It is a code of practice agreed by the advertising industry and the media, and anyone who advertises *must* comply with it. If your ad contravenes the code, it will not be accepted for publication or transmission. BCAP is administered by the **Advertising Standards Authority** (ASA). There are six main areas covered by BCAP which you need to be aware of.

- decency
- truthfulness
- health claims
- safety
- children
- environmental claims.

Decency

The code says that advertisements should contain nothing which is likely to cause grave or widespread offence, including causing offence on the grounds of race, religion, sex, sexual orientation or disability. The final arbiter of what is likely to cause offence is the ASA. If you are in doubt as to whether your own ad would fall into this category, consult the newspaper or magazine you are planning to advertise in (as they will have to decide whether or accept it or not), or

The Advertising Standards Authority
2–16 Torrington Place
London WC1E 7HN.

If your ad is accepted for publication ASA will probably only become involved if they receive a complaint from a member of the public. If they uphold the complaint, you will be asked to amend your ad; if you refuse you will find that it will no longer be accepted by the media.

Truth

Truth in advertising is slightly more complex.

- **Advertiser's licence** is acceptable when making subjective claims which cannot be quantified. For example, to advertise a book as

  The Best Book on the Subject

  is acceptable. The judgement of what is best is subjective, and it can't be substantiated. This is an acceptable piece of advertisers' licence. So terms like 'enormous savings', 'amazing value' or 'a beautiful design' can all be used, even if many readers do not agree with them.
  If, however, you were to say

  The Only Book to Cover the Syllabus

  you would have to able to substantiate your claim. Whether or not yours *is* the only book to cover the syllabus is something which can be proved to be truthful or not.

- **Prices** are of particular concern when considering the truthfulness of advertising. If you show prices in your ad, then it must be clear what they refer to. If you quote a price for a set of tea cups, but illustrate the whole set, including the teapot, sugar bowl and milk jug, then you must make it clear that only the cups are included in the price. Another stipulation is that if prices do not include VAT, then that fact must be stated as prominently as the price itself.

- **Testimonials**, in which someone endorses your product, are another area that can cause problems. Any testimonial must refer to the product you are advertising. If you change the product in any way, then the original testimonial is no long valid. The testimonial must also be truthful in itself. If you need a telescope to see the sea from your hotel, you cannot say

  'Sunnyside Hotel has Extensive Sea Views' – Mr Peter Brown.

  Even if Mr Brown *did* say it, it is not truthful, so you cannot use his quote. You also need the permission of the person concerned before you can use their name. Even if a famous film star uses your hairdressing salon, you cannot say so in your advertising without their permission.

Health claims

If you are advertising anything offering health benefits you should consult the ASA for advice. BCAP is particularly strict in this regard;

it has a list of diseases and conditions for which advertising is not allowed, and provision for a number of specific claims, including the prohibition of celebrity endorsement of medicines and restrictions on the way slimming products are advertised.

Safety

There are several safety provisions in BCAP, particularly relating to alcohol and motoring advertisements. For example, speed should not be portrayed in such a way as to encourage people to break the law, and alcohol advertisements should not encourage drinking and driving or suggest that the effects of alcohol can be masked in some way.

Children

There are restrictions on advertisements which encourage children to make excessive purchases, or which promote unhealthy eating habits such as 'snacking' or eating too many sweets. You may not advertise alcoholic drinks in a medium if more than twenty-five per cent of its audience is under 18.

Environmental claims

Claims such as 'environmentally friendly' should not be used without qualification unless there is convincing evidence that the product will cause no environmental damage. Moreover, if your product has never had any adverse effect on the environment, you cannot claim to have changed the formula to make it environmentally friendly.

OTHER VOLUNTARY ARRANGEMENTS

There are two other voluntary arrangements which concern specific areas of advertising. These are:

- the **Mail Order Protection Scheme**
- the **British Code of Sales Promotion Practice**.

The Mail Order Protection Scheme (MOPS)

This exists to protect the public against unscrupulous traders using direct response advertising to collect money, and then disappearing without supplying the goods. If you are planning to place a direct response ad, you will be required to complete an application form so that your credentials can be checked.

You may also be asked to furnish an **indemnity**. This means that you will have to deposit a certain sum of money, so that if you fail to supply goods for which a customer has paid, or if you refuse to issue a refund for goods returned, then your indemnity will be used to make those payments.

BCAP also requires direct response advertisers to:

- hold adequate stocks of their product before advertising

- fulfil orders normally within thirty days

- accept returns of undamaged goods within seven days.

The British Code of Sales Promotion Practice (BCSPP)

This Code is also administered by the ASA. It controls sales promotion schemes – premium gift offers, free gifts, vouchers, competitions, draws, etc. Most of the Code is straightforward – it simply requires that promotions should be:

- fair
- honest
- truthful.

However, there are very specific requirements for the wording of promotions, and for the conduct of competitions. So if you are planning to use such a scheme in your advertising, you should contact the ASA to ensure that what you have in mind is acceptable.

CHECKLIST

- Which of the various functions involved in producing an advertisement do you think you can perform yourself, and which do you think will have to be done by experts?

- Are you happy with the amount you are budgeting to spend on advertising? If it is less than one per cent or more than three per cent of your turnover, is there a good reason?

- Are you budgeting for and planning a year's advertising so as to have some cohesion to your campaign?

- Do you fully understand your obligations under the Sale of Goods Act, the Trade Descriptions Act and the three voluntary codes – the British Code of Advertising Practice, the Mail Order Protection Scheme and the British Code of Sales Promotion Practice?

3
Choosing the Right Media

The media (plural of medium) are the *means* by which a message is communicated – in this case your advertisement. It covers the news media (newspapers, magazines, TV, radio), but also includes non-news media such as poster sites and mailing lists.

Radio and television advertising require special techniques and equipment, and are not included in this survey of media available to the small business or local organisation. Contact your local commercial radio or TV station for advice if you want to use them.

CHOICE OF MEDIA

Apart from these, there are seven other main categories of advertising media. They are:

- national newspapers

- local newspapers

- specialist and trade publications

- outdoor advertising

- transport advertising

- local directories

- direct mail.

Take your time

Choosing the right media – and mix of media, because a combination of more than one is very often desirable – is vital if you are to get the most out of your advertising. Take your time over deciding which to use. Don't rush the decision, and don't allow yourself to be rushed by advertising sales people. It is their job to sell as much space as possible. It is yours to ensure that you take the right space in the right media, so in your own interests consider all the alternatives carefully.

More than one medium or more than one ad?

You could find that a combination of media, or of different types of ad, is what you need. It has been shown, for example, that if you want to get your name remembered, you need a whole series of ads to do it. One or two ads might make an immediate impact, but they will soon be forgotten. If you can't afford a lot of space on a regular basis but have quite a lot to say, therefore, you might consider taking two or three large ads a year. You can then explain your product in detail, and supplement them with smaller 'reminder' ads, either in the press or in the form of posters, to maintain public awareness.

Another way of avoiding the expense of a lot of large, costly, colourful ads is to place a series of small ads in the press inviting people to write in for more information; you can then send a brochure to those who respond. In that way, you will be spending most of your money on those who are genuinely interested.

Media buyers

There are specialist **media buyers**, but you may have to go some way to find one, as they are not very common – most media buyers are employed by advertising agencies. Unless you have very complex requirements, or are planning to spend thousands of pounds on advertising, it is probably not worth employing a media buyer. Although they can sometimes get you preferential rates, it is only feasible if you are putting a lot of business their way. For most small business people, it is one function they can very easily perform themselves. If you do decide to use a media buyer, contact:

The Association of Media Independents
48 Perry Road
London N12 8BU

for a list of their members.

NATIONAL NEWSPAPERS

Advertising in national newspapers is suitable for

● businesses with a very general, national market

and unsuitable for

• local businesses

• businesses with a national but specialist market.

Advertising in the national newspapers is very expensive. It represents good value in terms of the cost per reader, but the overall cost is high, as you are paying to reach a very wide audience, only a small percentage of whom are likely to be interested in your product. Some papers print regionally, and so can accept cheaper regional advertising, but it is still expensive.

So unless you have a product which is likely to appeal to all the readers of a particular paper throughout the country or region (and have a very large advertising budget!), steer clear of them. There are probably other media you could use to better effect.

If you are sure that national advertising *is* what you need, contact the newspapers of your choice for a **rate card**. This will give you all the information you need about rates, copy dates, etc. (See pp 39 for more on rate cards.)

LOCAL NEWSPAPERS

If your market is purely local or regional, then the local press is your best bet for advertising. This can be a daily or weekly paper for which you pay, or one of the many free newspapers which are now widely distributed.

Advertising in local papers is suitable for

• local businesses with a local market

and unsuitable for

• businesses or organisations with a national audience

• businesses or services which want customers to have a permanent record of their address or telephone number.

A daily or weekly paper?

If you have a choice between advertising in a daily or a weekly local paper, which will suit your needs best? With a daily newspaper you can ensure that people see your ad on a *particular day*, which can be a significant advantage. On the other hand, a daily newspaper is thrown out at the end of the day, whereas other media are more long-lasting, and may remain 'current' for a week or more.

Daily papers very often reach a wider area than weekly ones, so it would be worth asking each paper's advertising manager exactly which towns his or her paper covers.

A 'real' or free paper?

Your decision whether to use a free paper or one which readers have to pay for will largely depend on the quality of each in your own area. Free newspapers are usually distributed to *all* homes in their area, and so reach a wider audience than the 'real' ones, which are taken only by those who want them and are prepared to pay for them. On the other hand, papers for which people have paid tend to be taken more seriously. They usually contain more news, and are read more thoroughly; the free papers might be discarded without a second glance.

Buying space

The basic unit of space in a newspaper is the **single column centimetre** (scc). This is a space one column across and one centimetre deep. Some papers may have special rates for half- and quarter-pages, and you must expect to pay extra if you want to choose where your ad will appear. There are certain positions which, because of their prominence, are especially desirable, and therefore more expensive than most. In your local paper, these might be:

- front page title corner – the top corner next to the title of the paper

- front page solus (**solus** means it is the only ad on the page)

- TV page

- back page, next to the crossword.

It might be worth paying the extra to choose your position, either to give your ad more prominence or to ensure that it is read by the people you want to reach. A sports shop, for example, would do well to pay extra for their ad to appear on one of the sports pages; a garden centre would want to be near the gardening tips, and so on.

If you contact your local paper, their advertising staff will give you the rates for various sizes of ad, and advise you on presentation.

Classified ads

A useful, and quite cheap, way for small businesses to advertise is through **classified advertisements**. The classified columns of local newspapers are divided into a number of categories – properties, services, for sale and many more. Space is sold by the line for ordinary ads, with special rates for boxed ads, or ads with a design – *ie* not just straightforward text. Because classified ads are small, and nearly all text, it is vitally important to be concise and make every single word count.

CASE STUDY

Mary plans her advertising budget

Mary Davies has little difficulty choosing the media for her advertising. She decides to do the bulk in her local weekly newspaper, the *Merchester Herald*. She consider the free paper, but decides against it in the end on the grounds that most of her target audience will buy the *Herald* and discard the free sheet, which is very poor, both in quality and content. She therefore decides to allow for large ads in the *Herald*, 2 columns x 15 cm, in mid-June, early September and early December, to catch the summer reading, winter hobby/back-to-school and Christmas markets. In order to keep her shop in the public's mind, she also takes the small space next to the paper's title once a month, apart from the months in which she has a big ad.

This takes £875 of her £1,250 budget, and she uses the rest to advertise in a nearby town. Picton is only six miles from Merchester, and Mary wants to attract book-buyers from there to her shop. She therefore allocates £125 each for three 2 column x 10 cm ads in the *Picton Times*, to appear at about the same time as her main promotions.

SPECIALIST AND TRADE PUBLICATIONS

Specialist magazines are usually sold nationally (although there are some regional ones) and cover a wide range of leisure and other interests and hobbies, as well as many of the professions. If you want to reach architects, for example, or radio enthusiasts, or model makers, or any of a host of special interest groups, there will almost certainly be one or more magazines or journals in which you can advertise.

The trade press is sold just to members of particular trades, and is very useful for advertising to retailers – telling them about your promotional plans, what display material you have available etc., and generally encouraging them to stock your product.

Advertising in specialist publications is suitable for

- businesses or organisations with a national audience in a particular field

- businesses offering a product or service to a particular trade or profession

and unsuitable for

- businesses with a general market.

Using *BRAD*

If you have been involved in your particular area of business for some time, you may already be aware of all the media which cover it. If you are new to it, you will need help. In fact, even those who think they know the media inside out can benefit from the occasional refresher course. An invaluable reference source for anyone buying media space, but particularly for those looking at specialist and trade magazines, is *British Rate and Data*, universally known by its initials *BRAD*.

BRAD lists virtually all magazines, local and national, under various classifications (there is a separate listing for newspapers). It gives their addresses, their advertising rates, including special rates for special positions, their size, and usually their circulation and readership profile. It even gives the names of the executives so that you know whom to contact. A typical entry is shown on page 38. *BRAD* is updated every month, and is very expensive to buy, so you would probably do best to look at it in your local library. The copy they have might be slightly out of date, but will probably be quite adequate for your purposes.

BRAD enables you to see what publications are available to reach the particular market you want, and gives you most of the information you need to compare them. Of particular interest in this regard are the target readership and the editorial profiles, which will help you to decide whether the magazine concerned is aimed at your target audience. If you want any further information, or if the copy of *BRAD* you've been using is rather old, you can still contact the publisher and obtain up-to-date information and a recent copy of the magazine.

Certification of publications

Look out for the **Audit Bureau of Circulations** (ABC) certification. This organisation provides an independent audit of the circulation of any publication which asks it to, so that advertisers *know* that the figures quoted are correct. Most reputable publications invite it to audit their figures.

There is a similar scheme for publications which are not sold through newsagents or to subscribers, such as those that are delivered or those that are available as complimentary copies in hotels and

Your Garden

GARDENING **ipc** magazines

YOUR GARDEN

Affiliations ABC PPA NRS
Publisher IPC Magazines Limited, King's Reach Tower, Stamford Street, London, SE1 9LS Tel 071-261 6649. Fax 071-261 5546.
Contacts Editor Graham Clarke. Group Advertisement Manager Peter Sheldrake. Production Executive Bob Allen.
Display Advertisement Sales Tel 071-261 6649.
Classified Advertisement Sales Tel 071-261 2910. Fax 071-261 6579.
Frequency Monthly — first week of preceding month
Price Single copy £1.60
Editorial Profile Accessible, advice and instruction with a source of inspiration for attaining new projects and ideas. A broad range of editorial
Circulation Jan-June 1994 ABC 122,267 (UK & Eire 121,884 overseas 383)

	Total	UK&Eire	Other Ctries
Newstrade total	112,727	112,345	382
pd full	112,455	112,073	382
pd <50%	272	272	0
Subs total	9,174	9,174	0
pd full	61	61	0
pd >50%	9,007	9,007	0
pd <50% >20%	106	106	0
Mltpl copy/sponsored sub	2	2	0
pd >50%	2	2	0
Non-controlled free total	364	363	1
by name	364	363	1

Readership
All Adults Total Readership 423,000 (3.7 readers per copy based on Jan-Dec 1993 ABC 115,066)

	A	B	C1	C2	D	E
Profile Index	49	116	103	96	108	81
Coverage %	0	1	1	1	1	1
Coverage '000	6	87	117	95	74	43
	15-24	25-34	35-44	45-54	55-64	65+
Profile Index	42	92	102	134	132	108
Coverage %	0	1	1	1	1	1
Coverage '000	29	77	71	87	69	89

All Men Total Readership 185,000

	A	B	C1	C2	D	E
Profile Index	57	105	102	88	113	111
Coverage %	0	1	1	1	1	1
Coverage '000	4	37	48	42	34	21
	15-24	25-34	35-44	45-54	55-64	65+
Profile Index	41	69	106	122	159	129
Coverage %	0	1	1	1	1	1
Coverage '000	13	26	34	36	37	39

All Women Total Readership 238,000

	A	B	C1	C2	D	E
Profile Index	42	127	103	105	103	63
Coverage %	0	1	1	1	1	1
Coverage '000	3	50	69	54	40	22
	15-24	25-34	35-44	45-54	55-64	65+
Profile Index	44	112	99	144	111	94
Coverage %	0	1	1	1	1	1
Coverage '000	16	50	38	51	32	50

Main Shoppers (Female) Total Readership 224,000

	A	B	C1	C2	D	E
Profile Index	45	129	103	111	96	63
Coverage %	1	1	1	1	1	1
Coverage '000	3	48	64	53	34	21
	15-24	25-34	35-44	45-54	55-64	65+
Profile Index	53	110	91	128	105	91
Coverage %	1	1	1	1	1	1
Coverage '000	9	50	37	48	32	47

Main Shoppers (Total) Total Readership 303,000

	A	B	C1	C2	D	E
Profile Index	62	125	94	112	100	71
Coverage %	1	1	1	1	1	1
Coverage '000	5	66	78	73	48	32
	15-24	25-34	35-44	45-54	55-64	65+
Profile Index	46	88	101	128	123	97
Coverage %	0	1	1	1	1	1
Coverage '000	12	58	55	62	50	66

Source: NRS July 1993-June 1994 National Readership Surveys Limited
Target Readership Men and women aged 35-55 who are experienced but active amateur gardeners. Socio economic group of BC1/C2
Rates Effective 1 March 1994 Agency Commission 15%
Standard Rates
mono page £1180.00
colour page £1650.00
Mono Rates Mono: Page rop £1180.00, Half rop £630.00, Quarter rop £330.00, Eighth rop £180.00
Cover Rates Full colour: outside back £2062.50, 1 standard spot colour: outside back £1700.00 Mono: outside back £1340.00 series 6 — 5% extra 12 — 10% extra
Colour Rates Full colour: Page rop £1650.00, Half rop £880.00, 1 standard spot colour: Page rop £1430.00 Half page rop £770.00
Bleed Pages 10% extra
Special Positions rop 10% extra
Inserts Accepted by arrangement
Classified Rates box numbers £10.00 extra
Production Specifications Type area page 263 x 188, half portrait 263 x 92, half landscape 129 x 188, quarter portrait 129 x 92, eighth landscape 63 x 92, eighth portrait 129 x 44. Bleed size page 303 x 219. Trim size page 297 x 216. No of cols 4, 1 col 46, 2 cols 96, 3 cols 146 4 cols 196, length 263. Mono 40, colour 48. Heat Web Offset Litho.
Deadlines Copy — Colour — 35 days, mono 28 days preceding publication date. Cancellation — Colour — 6 months, mono 1 month prior to on sale date

Fig. 2. A typical *BRAD* entry (Source: *BRAD*).

aeroplanes. They can be certified by **Verified Free Distribution** (VFD).

Any publication whose circulation is not certified should be treated with a degree of caution. There may be good reasons why it has not been certified, but if you have to choose between two publications of apparently equal value as an advertising medium, stick to the one with the certified circulation. At least you can be certain that the figure quoted is an actual circulation figure.

Cost per thousand circulation

Armed with the advertising rates and the circulation figures, you can compare two similar publications in terms of advertising cost per thousand circulation.

Example
A quarter-page in publication A costs £175, and the circulation is 30,000. The same space in publication B costs £150, but the circulation is only 20,000. Which is a better deal?

Publication A: £175 for 30,000 = £5.83 per thousand
Publication B: £150 for 20,000 = £7.50 per thousand

So publication A gives a better deal.

The readership profile

The **readership profile** could also be of help in deciding which of several publications to use. Most publications have analysed their readership quite carefully, and show what proportion fall into each of the standard socio-economic categories. These categories are:

A   Top business people and leaders
B   Senior executives and managers
C1   White-collar clerical workers
C2   Skilled workers
D   Semi-skilled and unskilled workers
E   Poor pensioners, the disabled, casual workers.

If you wanted to reach not just anglers but anglers who were also senior executives, you would choose the angling magazine with the highest percentage of A and B readers. If your appeal was more to manual workers, you would go for the one with the most C2 and D readers.

Editorial profile

Finally, of course, you need to know the editorial content. This can be important, as the title will not always give a good indication of its

Playtime Games Ltd

45 BANKSIDE, RIVERVIEW INDUSTRIAL ESTATE,
NEWTOWN NT1 2AA
Tel: 01345 6789

12 May 199X

Worldwide Publications plc
Worldwide House
London EC1X ZY2

PURCHASE ORDER

Please reserve:	Advertising space in the November issue of LUDO NEWS
Position:	Right-hand page
Size:	Quarter-page (130 x 90mm)
Colour:	Mono
We supply:	Camera ready artwork
Date:	Artwork to be supplied to you by 14 October 199X
Price:	£200 exc VAT as quoted by you, 9 May 199X

With compliments

[*Signature*]

John Smith
Director

Fig. 3. An example of a space order.

particular bias. You cannot tell from the title, for example, whether a magazine entitled *Computer World* is aimed at the popular home computer market or the high-level professional. Similarly with a craft publication; is it aimed at the beginner or the more expert worker?

Reserving space
Once you have decided on the publication or publications which best suit your needs, and have decided on the space you want (see below), you can reserve your space. An example of a space order is shown in Fig. 3. Remember that if you want a special position, you will have to reserve your space well in advance. Special positions usually cost more, but will be seen by most readers. Exactly where these positions are will depend on the particular publication, but the most usual are:

- next to the contents column

- the inside front or back cover

- the outside back cover

- the first right-hand page of advertising

- next to editorial matter.

Many specialist magazines have classified columns, and this can be a good way for a small business to advertise. In the case study, for example, the Talbots choose to advertise initially under 'Holidays' in the classified section of the equestrian press. As with the local press, it is important to get the words rights, and to make it concise.

CASE STUDIES

The riding centre
The Talbots have considered several magazines for their advertisements, but many of them have uncertified circulations, and are rejected for that reason. From their own experience and from the readership profiles, they know that the weekly *Horse and Hound* and the fortnightly *Horse and Pony* reach complementary markets, and provide good value in terms of cost per thousand. These are therefore their primary publications. They plan to take an eighth of a page in the holiday sections of these two publications throughout January and February and again in October and November. They also decide to try an ad in *Pony Monthly*, a magazine with an uncertified circulation,

because they are keen to attract the younger market.

They have records of past customers going back several years, and have compiled a list of their addresses to mail their brochure to. They have also looked around for a mailing list to buy in. They discover that there is an Equestrian Book Society, whose members are keen riders and make up the sort of market profile the Talbots are looking for.

They can either rent a list of past members – 12,000 of them at £75 per thousand – or they can have their brochure inserted into one of the book society's own mailings to current members. In that way they can reach 18,000 people at £55 per thousand. They initially have doubts about letting the brochure go out with the society's own mailings, in case some of its impact is lost. On balance, however, they decide that reaching more people for less money (taking account of the fact that they would have to pay the postage on mailings to the past members list) outweighs any disadvantages. They also see a possible advantage in that the members will not discard a mailing from their book club without looking at it, which they might do with something from an unknown organisation.

They decide on a **roll-fold** brochure (A4 paper folded twice to provide six sides) as being economical, yet giving them enough space to work with.

The video makers

Vidco looked at *BRAD* to see what golfing media are available. They are surprised at how many publications there are, and realise that they can't advertise in all of them. Only three, however, have ABC certified circulations – *Fore!*, *Golf Monthly* and *Golf World*. *Golf Monthly* and *Golf World* offer the best value for money, as well as having the highest circulation, and the editorial content seems right for Vidco's market. *Fore!* has a lower circulation, and is more expensive in terms of cost per thousand, so they decide to use it less frequently than the other two.

These are therefore the three magazines in which Vidco will be advertising throughout the winter. *Golf Monthly* and *Golf World* are both monthly magazines, and they plan to take a quarter of a page in each issue from October to March. They will use *Fore!* just three times, at two-monthly intervals.

They also decide to test *Golf Weekly* with one ad in November, as although it is not ABC certified, its readership profile fits their potential market. If that proves successful, they will follow it up with further ads later. They will run a test ad in one of the other uncertified publications in February. They will also run a test in the summer, to see whether it is possible to sell instructional videos in the playing season. They decide on the June issue of *Golf Monthly* for this.

INSERTS

Another way of advertising in specialist publications is through **inserts** – brochures inserted into magazines. *BRAD* will tell you how much a publication charges for inserts. In this case, you have the brochures printed and delivered to the magazine. Inserts enable you to devote more space to your product than is possible with a page ad, and you can also use the same brochure in a number of different ways:

● as an insert

● in direct mail

● as a hand-out.

Inserts have both advantages and disadvantages over page ads. It is easy to throw an insert away as soon as you buy a magazine, whereas a page ad is there all the time. On the other hand, a well-designed insert is often more eye-catching, and it gives you more space to play with.

The printing of enough inserts to cover the whole circulation of one publication can be expensive. If you believe that inserts are right for you, it would probably pay to save your budget and do one extensive campaign in a number of media. By increasing your print run in this way, you would reduce the cost of each brochure, and therefore the cost of each insertion.

OUTDOOR ADVERTISING

Advertising outdoors is suitable for

● advertisers whose message is short

● top-up advertising to supplement a longer message in a press or television ad

and unsuitable for

● complex advertisements

● businesses with a product which appeals to a very specialist market – they will be reaching a general local audience, not a specialist national one.

Outdoor poster sites vary enormously both in their effectiveness and in their position. They can be on the roadside, on bus shelters, at sports fields, or in shopping centres. (Shopping centres are not strictly speaking outdoor sites, but their use as an advertising medium is the same as for 'true' outdoor advertising.)

The importance of location

If you want to use posters, choose your site with care. If you get the right site, it can be extremely effective, but the wrong site can be disastrous. A rugby pitch could be ideal for advertising sports goods, for example, but less effective for women's fashions! Similarly, a shopping centre site would be less effective if what you were advertising was not actually available in that centre.

One major advantage of posters is that you can **localise** your advertising, right down to the street corner on which you want it to appear. But outdoor posters are read 'on the move', whether on foot or in the car, so you must be able to communicate your message quickly. There is no time for a lot of copy or a long message. Even at sports fields, where the audience is the spectators rather than the players, the message should be short; people are there to watch the match not to read advertisements, and will only notice your poster in passing. It should ideally be no more than a picture and a slogan, which means that both must be first-rate for the poster to be effective.

Roadside posters

Roadside posters are measured in **sheets**, and usually range from four sheets (60 in x 40 in) to 48 sheets (10 ft x 20 ft). Because of their size, there may be special considerations to take into account in the design of your posters. What works as a quarter of a page will not necessarily work as a 48-sheet poster. You would do well to employ a professional designer if you are contemplating using posters.

If you are interested in a particular site, check the hoarding to see who owns it. For a sports field contact the club concerned; for a shopping centre the local council will be able to advise you. Some ninety per cent of roadside sites are owned by members of the **Outdoor Advertising Association of Great Britain**, and they would be able to give you useful advice. Their address is

Outdoor Advertising Association of Great Britain
77 Newman Street
London W1A 1DX
Tel: (0171) 637 7703.

TRANSPORT ADVERTISING

Transport advertising is suitable for

- organisations trying to reach specific groups who use buses or trains – shoppers or schoolchildren on buses, for example, or commuters at stations

- local businesses with a local market

and unsuitable for

- businesses with a specialist market

- organisations trying to reach people who do not generally use public transport.

Transport advertising includes bus and Underground advertising and posters in stations. Buses offer opportunities for posters both outside and inside. Advertisements on the outsides of buses are very similar to the outdoor advertising described above. They are seen 'on the move', and need to make an immediate impact, with a quickly grasped message. You cannot localise them in the way you can on fixed sites, but this could in fact be an advantage – buses could carry your message to a wide area.

Ads inside transport

Inside buses or the Underground your message can be more detailed. There is time for passengers to read the advertisements – in fact, in many cases they have nothing else to do! It is often cheaper to advertise inside a bus than on the outside, too. The only constraint is the size and shape of the space available for advertising.

Your local bus company will tell you who handles their advertising. The railway company will advise you on station advertising.

Unlike hoardings, posters on buses and stations come in all shapes and sizes, and you will need to consult the bus or railway company about their requirements as well as the cost.

LOCAL DIRECTORIES

Advertising in local directories is suitable for

- local businesses with a local market

- 'permanent' advertising to which the customer can refer at any time

and unsuitable for

- businesses with a national market

- businesses which do not fall easily into any of the directory classifications.

Probably the best-known local directory is *Yellow Pages*, but there are others, such as *Thomson Local Directory* and *Telepages*.

Some businesses derive more benefit from local directories than others; much depends on whether yours is a service or shop for which people generally refer to them. An electrician can benefit greatly from an advertisement in a local directory, because that is one of the first places people look if they need electrical work done. A department store will do less well, because the public usually turn to local directories for more *specific* needs.

Types of ad

You can stick to a standard entry, but if you do, you risk being lost among the display ads in your category. Look up your own category in one of the directories and see how many display ads there are. If there are very few in relation to the total number of entries, then you may be all right with just a standard entry. If there are a lot of display ads, then seriously consider taking one yourself.

What to avoid

There are one or two restrictions on the way you advertise in local directories. First, it's not wise to use photographs; they won't reproduce well on the cheap and often coloured paper the directories use, and will make your ad look messy. Secondly, don't forget that an ad in a local directory lasts for a whole year. So any seasonal references will look odd in the 'off' season. Thirdly, bear in mind that people looking in a local directory are already aware that they have a need. You don't have to waste time telling them that toys make good presents – if they are looking under 'Toy and game shops' in *Yellow Pages* they already know that. You need to persuade them that they should buy their toys only from *you*. And fourthly, people are generally looking for a shop or service in their particular area, so indicate where you are clearly and boldly.

Bear in mind, too, that only *Yellow Pages* is delivered to businesses. The other directories go only to homes, and would be little use for advertising to other businesses.

CASE STUDY

The plumber

Peter Jackson finds that his £750 will buy him a standard 2½-inch square ad in *Yellow Pages*, with smaller ads in *Thompson* and *Telepages*. He goes for smaller ads in these two because everyone else's ads are smaller, so his will not have to compete so hard. He has enough left over for a 2 column x 5cm ad in his local paper in May, June, July, August and September. He also decides to write a sales letter to about fifty building contractors in his area, quoting his former employer as a reference for the quality of his work, and asking them to bear him in mind for any subcontract work that might be available.

DIRECT MAIL

Direct mail is suitable for

- organisations wanting to reach a well-defined audience, whether geographically, economically or socially

- organisations whose message is long, or needs a lot of illustration

- advertising which needs to be seen at a specific time – as in the launch of a new business, or to tie in with a particular event

and unsuitable for

- very general advertising

- organisations with a very short message.

Direct mail is the distribution of advertising material direct to people's addresses, whether the postal service is actually used or not. The mailing piece can be as large as you like – within reason of course – so it is a very versatile medium. You can target your market rather better than you can in most other forms of advertising by using very specific mailing lists. Indeed, if your mailing piece is a sales letter, then a short, very specific, mailing list is almost essential.

If you are launching a new local business, then distributing a small leaflet in the right area is a very good way of getting your name known – especially if it includes a device like a money-off voucher to encourage the public to come and see the business themselves.

Obtaining a mailing list

There are a number of ways in which you can get a mailing list.

- If you want repeat business, you can use your own customer files. Be sure to 'clean' the list from time to time to remove people who have moved or who were bad debts.

- You can compile your own list from *Yellow Pages* or professional directories if you want people in a particular line of business, or from the electoral roll for people in a particular area. *Yellow Pages* is a particularly good source if you are doing a sales letter.

- You can rent a list from a **list broker** – someone who specialises in compiling mailing lists. Look under 'Direct mail' in *Yellow Pages* or write to
    The Direct Marketing Association (UK) Ltd
    Haymarket House
    1 Oxenden Street
    London SW17 4EE
    Tel: (0171) 321 2525.

- You can approach organisations like professional institutions, credit card companies, mail order companies or book clubs – anyone who does a lot of mailing themselves. Some will rent their lists, others won't.

Your local postal sales representative will advise you on mailing lists generally, and tell you of the Post Office's special schemes and postal rates for large mailings. Contact him or her at the nearest Business Services section of the Post Office (look under Post Office in the phone book).

If you rent a mailing list, you are only entitled to use it once. Don't be tempted to use it more than once without paying. The list broker will almost certainly have one or more 'check addresses' in the list (perhaps the homes of employees), and will very soon find out if you try to cheat the system.

Sales letters

A special form of direct mail is the sales letter. Like a brochure, it is mailed to your prospective customer, but it should be personalised and individually addressed. This only works if your mailing list is relatively short – say 100 addresses or less – and is best for business-to-business advertising.

Distribution

You can send your brochures through the mail; that is obviously the best way of distribution if your potential clients are scattered around the country rather than concentrated in one or two particular areas. If you have a particular area you want covered, however (as with the launch of a new local business), you may find a leaflet distributor better value. Look under 'Circular & sample distributors' in *Yellow Pages*. These are also specialist mailing houses which will take over the whole organisation of your direct mail operation for a fee. Look under 'Direct mail' in *Yellow Pages*.

Cost

Printing is by far the largest cost element in direct mail. So, before you start, make sure you know what it is likely to cost to have your brochure printed. You will not be able to get a firm estimate from a printer until you can give him a definite idea of illustrations, layout, size etc. But most firms will be happy to give you a rough idea of the sort of costs involved, so that you can budget and decide on your mailing lists. For more on dealing with printers, see chapter 9.

As the case studies show, most advertising campaigns use a number of different media. Choosing what combination you need is not easy, but now you know what each one involves, have a look at the flow chart in Fig. 4 which provides a simple aid to making the decision.

HOW MUCH SPACE DO I NEED?

Before you can answer this questions, you need to ask yourself four others:

- How much space can I afford?

- How much have I got to say?

- How many ads do I need?

- What medium am I using?

It is these four criteria, and their permutations, that will decide how much space you take.

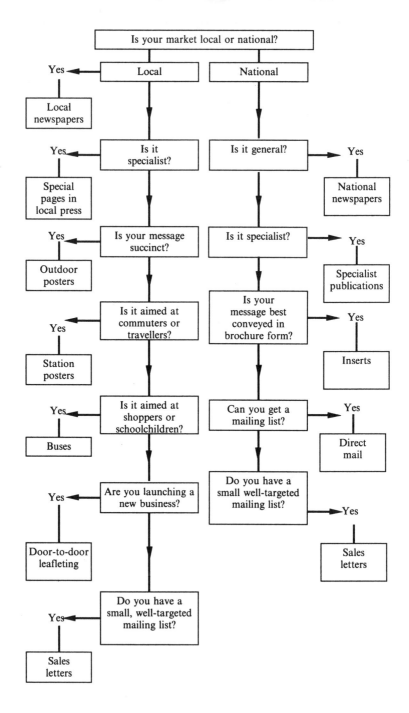

Fig. 4. A guide through the media maze.

How much can I afford?

However you set your advertising budget, it is unlikely to be completely open-ended. Even if you started with how much you need to spend, as suggested in chapter 1, you will have considered what that represents as a proportion of turnover, and perhaps reassessed your needs accordingly. You may find yourself having to choose between various combinations of large and small ads. That is when you have to ask yourself the second and third questions.

Large ads or small?

If your message is short, it might be best to place a series of relatively small but prominent ads in more than one place. On the other hand, if there is really only one newspaper or magazine from which you believe you will get a good response, you would do better to place a large ad in that one than to dissipate your effort in marginal publications.

If the purpose of your campaign is to make your product known, then a series of ads in the same publication is the best way to do it – one ad alone will not make you a household name. On the other hand, if yours is a direct response ad, with the sole purpose of eliciting orders there and then, making your product known in a more general sense is not so important.

There is no 'best' size for an ad. Obviously, the larger it is, the more chance it has of being noticed. But size is not everything – a full-page ad is not necessarily twice as effective as a half-page one. The relationship between the size and cost of the space and the response you can expect will vary according to the publication, the position, and what it is you are advertising.

As a general rule, try not to skimp on space. If you need to say a lot about your product, don't try to cram it all into a small ad. Readers will just pass it by. It might be better to wait and place one ad of the right size less frequently. A large ad every two months would probably yield better results than a small one every week.

Rules were made to be broken, however, particularly in advertising. There will be occasions or products for which it is necessary to place a series of ads, even if it means making them smaller than you would like. As we have said, this is particularly true when you want to get your product known, to get people to ask for it when they go shopping. One way to get something of the best of both worlds is to place one large ad, in which you can set out all the benefits, followed by a series of small ones, in which you just plug away at the slogan or headline. In this way you have the advantage of being able to say everything you need to, while still being able to keep your name in the public eye. This can be done either by a large ad in the local paper followed by a series of small ads (as Mary Davies decided to do for her bookshop) or by a newspaper ad backed up by a poster campaign.

The only way you can really find the size and frequency that is best for you, however, is by trial and error – or perhaps by copying your more established rivals, who will hopefully have done the trail and error already!

Be appropriate

There are certain media which almost dictate the size themselves. For example, a display ad in a local directory will not be very big, nor will it need to say much. After all, if people are looking under 'Plumbers' in *Yellow Pages*, it is for a reason. You don't have to attract their attention in the way that you would if they were just thumbing through a newspaper. What you have to do is to persuade them that *you* are the plumber they need.

BROCHURES

While considering the question of space, we should look in particular at brochures. The main advantage is obvious – you can vary the size of your brochure according to the amount of space you need to get your message across. The possibilities are not limitless, however. Apart from cost, you will find yourself restricted by the standard paper sizes, and by the fact that the size of a brochure can usually only go up in multiples of four pages.

Size

The most common page sizes for brochures are A4 and A5. A4 is 297 x 210 millimetres, and A5 half this size (about 210 x 149 millimetres). A5 is probably the more popular, certainly for mailing. Any 'odd' sizes – those that do not conform to the standard 'A' series system – would be more expensive. You would have to buy the next biggest standard size of paper, and trim it to size, which would be both costly and wasteful.

Layout

There are various ways in which a brochure can be laid out:

- The simplest is a single sheet – two sides.

- The next simplest is one sheet, folded to give four sides, for example A3 folded to A4 or A4 folded to A5.

- To get six sides, you can fold a sheet twice, as in Fig. 5. This is called a **roll-fold**.

- The standard format for eight sides is two sheets folded and stapled (sometimes called wire-stitched).

- A different way of achieving eight sides is a **gate-fold**. For this you fold a sheet three times, as in the second diagram in Fig. 5. This gives a rather elongated look to the brochure.

For anything larger than eight sides, you would continue to add sheets to the stapled format, so that your brochure would go up from eight to twelve to sixteen pages. As with space ads and posters, however, the larger the size, the more expensive it will be, so you should get a written estimate of all the costs before you go too far.

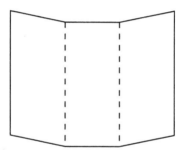

A roll-fold brochure.

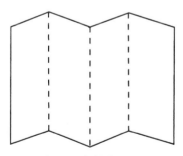

A gate-fold brochure.

Fig. 5. Brochure layouts.

CHECKLIST

- Have you considered the media options carefully or are you being rushed into a decision?

- Is your product general enough and your budget large enough to justify advertising in national newspapers?

- If you have a specialist product, are you advertising on a specialist page of a paper or in a specialist magazine?

- Do you know how to use *BRAD*, and how to compare different publications for value-for-money?

- If you need a lot of space to promote your product, have you considered an insert in magazines?

- Is your message short enough to make outdoor advertising viable?

- Will your product appeal to users of buses or trains?

- Are you able to compile a mailing list to do a direct mail shot?

- Do you have a small, well-targeted mailing list to send personalised sales letters to?

- Have you established the best size and frequency of advertisement for your business?

4
Planning the Right Advertisement

Now that you have decided what media you are going to use and how much you have to spend, you can move on to the next – and probably the most important – stage: the advertising **brief**. This is when the client tells the copywriter and designer about the product, and about the approach he wants to take in the ad or campaign, bearing in mind any competitors. Advertising agencies spend a lot of time getting to know their client's product; and this element is just as important when you are doing the whole job yourself.

- Always write down a thorough brief, even if the person you are briefing is yourself.

Unless you prepare a proper *written* brief, the chances are that you will leave something important out. Now is also the time to start thinking of the type of ad you want – colour or black and white? Illustrated or not? Don't rely on your memory.

MARKET RESEARCH

Market research is usually concerned with sampling the public on their preferences; here we will use the term more loosely to signify the *whole* market – your product, those of your competitors, and your target audience.

Your product

How much do you really know about your product? When did you last see it actually being produced? If you are a retailer, do you know exactly what goes on on the shop floor? Do you run a hotel? If so, do you know *why* you do things the way you do, or is it just because 'it's always been done that way'?

What does all this have to do with advertising? Look at some of the ads in your daily paper. Many of them contain a lot of information – much of it technical. It is usually nicely written and presented, but

How well do you know your own product?

1. If you are a manufacturer, what materials do you use and why do you use them?

    ....

2. Do you have quality control checks? If so, what are they? If not, why not?

    ....

3. What processes and procedures do you go through in running your business, stage by stage?

    ....

4. If you are a retailer, why do you stock one supplier's goods and not another's?

    ....

5. Do you offer your customers any extra services such as special order facilities, free delivery or individual advice?

    ....

6. What sales pitch works best for your salesforce. (They are selling for you all the time, so they should know.)

    ....

7. If you provide a service, how and on what terms do you provide it?

    ....

8. Do your clients come to you, or do you go to them?

    ....

9. What procedures do you have for dealing with complaints from customers or clients?

    ....

10. Are there any extra charges?

    ....

Fig. 6. Your product questionnaire.

basically it is technical detail. Those ads appear because an advertising copywriter took the time to find out about the boring details and realised that they could be used as a way to demonstrate how good the products are.

I am not suggesting that you *must* go into this kind of detail about what you are advertising. But unless you know *all* about your product or service, how do you know which aspects of it are superior to those of your competitors? Use the questionnaire in Fig. 6 to check your knowledge of your business.

The list can be extended *ad infinitum*, depending on your particular business, but these are the most basic questions to ask yourself. There are no 'right' or 'wrong' answers, but the more you know about your product, the easier it will be to find something vital and positive to say about it. Don't worry if you end up with a mass of disjointed information. It will fall into place in due course!

The competition

Having got to know your own product or service inside out, you need to do the same with those of your rivals. Find out as much about *their* materials, processes, suppliers, methods, etc as possible. It is unlikely that you will be able to find out as much about them as you can about your own business, but get as close as you can. If they are manufacturers, visit some of the retailers they distribute through and get them to give you the sales pitch. If they provide a service, speak to some of their clients. Once again, your own sales force should be able to give you some feedback. There is nothing some customers like more than to tell a salesperson how much better their competitors are!

Find out what is good about them, and what is bad.

- Are they as cheap as you?

- Is their quality as high?

- Are they as meticulous in their procedures?

- What benefits do you offer that your rivals don't?

- And what do *they* offer that *you* don't?

- Look carefully at their advertising. What do they themselves see as their strengths?

There may seem to be little to choose between what you and your rivals have to offer. That is no problem. Your ad doesn't have to compare the two, but at least by going through this exercise you will discover what advertising approaches are open to you.

Your market

What audience will your advertisement be aimed at? It is tempting to answer, 'Almost anyone will be interested in what I have to offer.' That is very seldom the case! Of course it is possible for a product, or more usually a service, to appeal to more than one kind of person. And you will undoubtedly achieve *some* sales to people you are not specifically aiming at. But it is very difficult to reach more than one *main* audience with one ad. So where there is genuinely more than one type of potential customer, you need to look at each individually as a separate audience, and plan separate ads.

An electrician is a case in point. He might be aiming at the householder, but also at the building trade – two very different markets for his service – and he won't reach them both effectively with one ad.

Be very clear in your mind who you would like to see responding to each ad – your **target audience**. Is it the people you already sell to? If so, it should be relatively easy to analyse them. But perhaps you are new to your particular field, or are trying to break into new markets. In that case, you need to have a clear picture of who you think you are selling to.

You know your product or service. Who would it appeal to? To put it another way, who did you have in mind when you established your business? The following questions will help you draw a profile of the sort of person you have in mind.

1. What is the age of your target audience?

2. Are they predominantly male or female?

3. What is their financial position?

4. What kind of areas do they live in?

5. What kind of jobs do they do?

6. Are they most attracted by price, service or quality?

7. What is their lifestyle?

8. What are their interests?

These are the basic questions to ask. Some will not be relevant to some businesses, and there will be others that specific businesses need to ask. Someone selling computer software will want to know what hardware their potential customers have; a camera shop might ask what their level of expertise is, and so on.

When you have this theoretical picture, try to visualise a particular person you know who fits it: Mrs X down the road, perhaps, or Mr Y, the Systems Manager at the engineering company on the industrial estate, or young Sally Z, who has just started at university. Keep that person in mind all the time you are putting together your ad, as though you were talking directly to them, and the chances are you will hit your target audience.

Planning direct mail

There is another aspect to targeting your audience, which arises in direct mail. When putting together a brochure, you not only need to visualise your customer, you also need to establish the *purpose* of the brochure. If it is to be distributed widely and fairly indiscriminately, in order to elicit enquiries, you may not want to spend a lot of money producing it. You may want to reserve the expensive production for the follow-up brochure to those who have responded and shown an interest. If on the other hand your *initial* mailing is to a specific, well-targeted group, then you can give your first brochure the full treatment.

This market research *is* important. Even if you do not use it directly in your advertising, you will find the information valuable in the running of your business. But don't rush it. Do it bit by bit, and allow time for the facts to sink into your subconscious – and for the most important ones to emerge again. You will begin to develop a clear and objective idea of where your product or service stands in relation to the competition and to the potential customers – what is termed its 'position' in the market.

WHAT BENEFITS DO YOU OFFER

You have studied your product, you have looked at your rivals, you have researched your market. You should now be ready to list all the benefits you offer – and do list *all* the benefits. Where you offer benefits that your competitors don't, make a note, but don't restrict yourself to those areas. Write down everything that should make people want to buy what you are offering.

Armed with the information gained in your market research, you should find it quite easy to draw up a list. Why should you make a list of benefits? Because you are not selling your *product* as such in an advertisement – you are selling the *benefits* it offers your customers. No one will buy a cooker just because it is a cooker. They will buy it because having one offers them certain benefits – the ability to bake or grill food, for example!

Once you have your list, try to put your benefits in order of importance. This is not always easy, because the timing of your ad has some bearing. As Mary Davies finds with her bookshop, something that is an important benefit at Christmas (books make good gifts, for example) becomes less important in summer. Moreover something that is vitally important to one person may not matter much to another. It will help you get the order right if you bear in mind the person you are trying to sell to.

The unique selling proposition

There is a concept in advertising called a **unique selling proposition** (USP). This is just jargon for something which makes your product or service special, something you have that your competitors don't. In the case of Mary Davies's bookshop, for example, the USP would be that it has the widest range of books on hobbies in the area.

If you have a USP, then use it. If you don't, consider whether you could introduce one. For example, a guarantee could be an invaluable USP. Wouldn't *you* be attracted by an ad that said:

Others *Tell* You Their (Product) Lasts Five Years
We *Guarantee* IT!

It might cost you a bit more in replacing or repairing faulty products, but the extra sales could more than compensate. Other examples of USPs that could be introduced are the 'never knowingly undersold' type guarantees, 24-hour delivery, or the addition of one more quality control check than the opposition.

If you don't have a USP and it would be expensive or difficult to introduce one, then don't try to force the issue. Concentrate on selling the benefits you *can* offer, or highlight a benefit which your competitors might also offer, but which they don't use in their advertising.

The emotional buying trigger

The concept of the USP has to a certain extent been superseded by the idea of **emotional buying triggers**. This is advertiser's jargon for appeals to your emotions and instincts. They need to feel loved, to be part of the 'in' crowd, to achieve, to feel secure, to be an individual, the instinct of survival – all can trigger a buying response if given the right stimulus: 'Care for *your* family's environment – choose the washing powder with the green whitener.'

YOUR IMAGE

Brand or **company image** can be important. You need to decide whether you want to project a particular image, and if so, what that image is. If you own a bakery, for example, do you want to project a traditional image, or one of gleaming modernity, or healthy wholesomeness? A restaurant may be trying to appeal to a sophisticated clientele or to the family trade. A dress manufacturer must decide whether he or she wants to attract the young buyer, the businesswoman, the fashion-conscious woman about town. In all these cases, an image has to be created.

This image can be projected in a number of ways, many of them quite subtle. We are all familiar with the images projected in television and national magazine ads, many of which have little or nothing to do with the product – the dinner party at which a certain brand of coffee is served, for example, which gives that coffee a distinctly sophisticated image. But image-creating does not have to be that obvious. The ad in Fig. 7 is a case in point. The impression the reader is left with is that these are clothes for the fashionable young woman about town, the modern woman with a busy lifestyle. Yet there is nothing explicitly stated. It is all a matter of *image*. The devices you can use are discussed in the next chapter, but first it is important to know what *your* image is to be.

It is not essential to have a particular image at all. Many advertisers manage quite well without one, but how you want to present yourself should form part of your brief.

CASE STUDIES

The bookshop
Mary Davies's bookshop specialises in books for hobbies and leisure interests, although she stocks quite a wide range of novels as well. She also makes sure that she stocks all the books recommended in the Adult Education Centre's evening classes. Her list of benefits runs like this:

- Widest range of practical leisure books in the area.

- All recommended evening class books stocked.

Dress with Style

Collections for
Winter in
sizes 10 to 22
at

The

Fashion House

THE COURTYARD, ST JAMES STREET,
TAUNTON, SOMERSET
TELEPHONE (0823) 331053

Fig. 7. An ad creating an image.

- Spacious, congenial shop, well lit and easy to find your way round.

- Plenty of good reading.

- Will order any book at no extra charge.

- Books make very good presents.

- Good range of school supplies, reference books and revision aids.

It is difficult to put these benefits in order of importance, because some of them will be more important at different times of the year. There is, however, one USP, which is that she has the widest range of practical leisure books in the area. She will probably not make this the most prominent item in all her ads, but it will certainly feature in all of them.

The riding centre

The Talbots' list of benefits is longer than those of the other businesses we are looking at. That doesn't matter – what is important is to get *all* benefits down, no matter how many or how few there are. Their benefits, in no particular order, are:

- Only five minutes from the sea.

- Mixed riding – lanes, open countryside, and of course the beach.

- Service is friendly.

- Reasonably priced.

- An indoor and an outdoor school, as well as a show-jumping arena.

- Self-catering accommodation is available.

- Beautiful views and walks, making it an ideal centre even for non-riders.

- Reliable, well-trained horses.

- Stabling available if you want to bring your own horse.

- Special courses arranged if required.

- All instructors are fully qualified.

The video makers
Vidco's list of benefits is relatively short. It runs like this:

- Improve your golf.

- Learn in the comfort of your own home.

- Tuition from the experts.

- It costs considerably less than professional lessons.

- The videos are of the highest quality.

- No-quibble money-back guarantee if you are not satisfied.

Although the list is short, there is a powerful emotional buying trigger there. It is the desire to excel, to improve your game of golf.

The plumber
Peter Jackson lists all the benefits he can offer, but when he comes to put them in order of importance he finds that because he is trying to reach different audiences, he has to have three lists: one for the local directories; a different one for his newspaper ads, where he will be aiming particularly at the central heating market; and a third for building contractors.

His list for the local directory, in order of importance, is:

- All work guaranteed.

- Reasonable rates.

- Member of the Institute of Plumbing.

- Fast service.

- Corgi registered gas installer.

- Handles all plumbing jobs, including repairs and blockages.

For the newspaper ads, the list is:

- All work guaranteed.

- Corgi registered gas installer.

- Reasonable rates.

- Member of the Institute of Plumbing.

- Fast service.

And for building contractors it is:

- Reasonable rates.

- Good timekeeper.

- Members of the Institute of Plumbing.

- Corgi registered gas installer.

- Handles all plumbing jobs.

ILLUSTRATING YOUR AD

Illustrations generally help an ad. They give it a lift, an added dimension. They are not essential, however. Some quite eye-catching effects are possible with just typography, as you can see in Fig. 11. Illustrations, of course, can be more expensive than just type. On the other hand, it is more difficult to design a really effective ad without them. As a general rule, if what you are advertising *can* be illustrated, it pays to do so. But rules are meant to be broken, and if you think you can put together a good ad without illustrations, give it a try.

Different uses for illustrations

Illustrations are not only used to depict a product, though. Even if what you are advertising may not easily be illustrated itself – a gardening service, for example, or a piece of computer software – an illustration can still be useful. It can convey **atmosphere** or show what benefits the product or service can supply. So the gardening service's ad could show an illustration of an immaculate garden, or the computer software manufacturer could show a program in action. A retired couple pictured on holiday or enjoying their hobbies could create an atmosphere in which to put across a message about a pensions adviser's services.

How many illustrations?

How many illustrations you use depends on how much space you have, and on what the illustrations are for. There is seldom any point in showing more than one 'atmospheric' picture, but you could combine that with a picture of the product – a girl in white running across a meadow to create the atmosphere, for example, together with a picture of the soap she is actually advertising. Usually one or two illustrations are sufficient, but there are times when more are necessary. If you are advertising a hotel, for example, you may need to illustrate a variety of views and facilities. With certain products, close-up shots may be necessary. If space is limited, too many pictures can give an ad a cluttered look, and you may find that you do not have enough room for the copy.

Examples

● Peter Jackson, the plumber, comes to the conclusion that he doesn't need any illustrations. His are small ads, he has nothing particular to show, and they would just clutter up the ad.

● Mary Davies, the bookseller, wants to illustrate her ads. She will have a photograph of a collection of appropriate books in each big ad.

● Vidco decide to illustrate the actual videos, and to include another illustration showing their effect, eg someone playing better golf.

● The Talbots will need plenty of illustrations for their riding centre brochure, probably two per page, but none for the small ads they place in the equestrian magazines. Like Peter Jackson they feel that any illustrations in those ads would simply clutter them up.

Illustrations can sometimes be used to break up long stretches of copy into 'digestible' chunks. How many you use in this way will depend on the copy itself, and any decision on this kind of illustration is probably best left until the layout stage.

ADVERTISING IN COLOUR

When to use colour

A colour ad is much more expensive than a black and white one – a quick look at the colour rates in *BRAD* will show you that. So when is colour appropriate? There are two questions to ask yourself.

• Is colour *necessary* to illustrate my product effectively?

• Does the image I want to project require the product to look *prestigious*?

If the answer to either of those questions is yes, you should seriously consider using colour. If the answer to *both* is yes, there should be no doubt in your mind. If the answer to both is no, then colour is probably going to be wasted. If you are selling a range of paints, for example, or a beautifully illustrated art book, it would be difficult to advertise them effectively in black and white. If, on the other hand, you are selling electrical supplies, a black and white ad will probably be just as effective as colour. A luxury hotel might need to be shown in colour to give it the right image, whereas a black and white ad could suit the local pub.

Colour in a brochure

A black and white brochure can very easily look boring. If you are doing a brochure which does not need the full colour treatment, you might consider using just two colours. A combination of a colour and black, with all the tints than can be achieved with that combination, can be very effective, especially if a tinted paper is also used.

It is best to stick to either two or four colours. (Virtually any shade can be created by mixing four basic colours in various combinations, so colour printing is usually done in those four colours – see chapter 8.) Three colours are possible, but the cost is almost as high as for four, and the effect is little different from two.

Of the case studies we are looking at, only the Talbots decide to use colour. Vidco toyed with the idea, but came to the conclusion that since they were not showing the videos themselves, just the covers, the expense of colour would not be justified. The Talbots, however, need colour in their brochure to convey the beauty of their position, and to create an up-market image.

WHAT IF THERE'S NOTHING TO SAY?

It is rare that a seller can find nothing to say about a product, or at least nothing relevant or interesting. Baked beans might be a case in point; what can you say about your baked beans that is interesting, or that is any different from everyone else's? If you are trying to advertise something like that, don't bore your audience by finding USPs that nobody's interested in. Look for another angle. Here are a few tips.

- Is there a **new way of using** your product – even something a bit bizarre? As long as it's not too way out, it could make people notice and remember the name.

- Try using **humour**. Funny advertisements are not easy to do, and can be rather risky, but they *can* work. Just remember your 'typical' buyer and gear your humour to him or her.

- Invent a **slogan**. Slogans are generally fairly meaningless, but if they catch on, they can ensure that your name sticks in people's subconscious. Guinness's 'Pure Genius', British Gas's 'Don't you love being in control?', BT's 'It's good to talk' – all of these tell us nothing about the product, but the very fact that people remember them means that they have been successful. But be warned: slogans only work if you are planning a series of ads. And even the experts don't get slogans right every time. You could coin a slogan that nobody remembers.

- Go for **atmosphere**. Set your baked beans in a charming old-fashioned kitchen, for example, with copy showing that they are made to the same traditional recipe as when they were first produced.

- Advertise the **product itself**, not your brand. Tell people how healthy baked beans are, and how much children like them – therefore what a help they are in giving children a healthy diet. People will soon associate the healthy aspects of baked beans with your brand.

ORGANISING CONTESTS

Contests can be used for two purposes.

- To attract people to look at your ad

- To help launch a new product.

Each type needs to be treated slightly differently. In the first instance, you will need to be able to offer a very special first prize (or a rather unusual one) otherwise you will not attract enough people's attention. A holiday in Barbados would be good, or a course of parachuting lessons – anything which will persuade people to give your ad more than a passing glance, whether they actually enter the contest or not. You should also ensure that the contest does not dominate what you are trying to advertise, otherwise it will defeat the whole object of the exercise.

The problem with this kind of contest is that if the main prize is going to be attractive enough, it is likely to be expensive. You would need to be very sure that the increase in sales resulting from the contest was enough to justify the expense.

If you are using a competition as a means of launching a new product, you should offer a large number of small prizes, and insist on **proof of purchase** of the product with every entry. With only a few prizes, no matter how attractive, many people will be put off entering because they don't believe that they have a chance of winning. That doesn't matter if your aim is just to make people read your ad. But if you are launching a product, then you want people to enter, so that they buy the product. The greater the number of prizes, the greater the chance of someone winning one, and so the greater the response. The proof of purchase actually makes them buy your product, and ensures that as many people as possible try it.

Contests and the law

If you are considering using a contest in your advertising, make sure that you fully understand the legal position. The British Code of Sales Promotion Practice, mentioned in Chapter 1, is a voluntary code of practice with which you should be familiar, but you should also consult a lawyer to ensure that you do not fall foul of the law.

STAGES OF YOUR BRIEF

If you write down your ideas as you work through the stages suggested above you should end up with some sort of written brief. What format you use is, of course, up to you, but the information may come under the following headings:

- Main market
- Other markets
- USP
- Emotional buying trigger
- Other benefits
- Image
- Space
- Illustrations
- Colour
- Using a contest.

CHECKLIST

- Have you prepared a thorough brief, even if you are doing the whole job yourself?

- Do you know as much as you should about your product, and those of your competitors?

- Do you know your target audience?

- What kind of image do you want to project?

- What benefits do you offer, and do you have a unique selling proposition or emotional buying trigger?

- How many illustrations do you need?

- Do you need colour?

- If you are going to use a contest in your ad, are you sure of your legal position?

5
Successful Layout Techniques

You should now have a good idea of your product, your market, the image you want to project, and the space you have to work with. You can move on to the actual design of the ad, and starting working on your **layout**. A layout, also called a **visual** or a **rough**, is a 'sketch' of what the ad will look like; it is drawn to the size and shape of the finished ad, with the position of each element clearly indicated.

Do-it-yourself or professional?

It is quite possible to lay out the ad yourself. All it needs is a little imagination, and a bit of guidance as to the techniques. If you want a complex ad, or if you want to compete with the big names, then a professional designer is essential (see chapter 9), but for a simple, straightforward layout there is no reason why, with a little practice, you can't put together a very effective ad yourself. You will need:

- A pencil

- Black pens of various thicknesses

- Paper. Many designers do the final layout on high-quality tracing paper, but ordinary drawing paper will do.

If you have a DTP system, you will be able to experiment with various layouts on your computer, but the basic principles are the same as for the pen and paper approach. A DTP system does *not* make you a designer. It is simply a tool like any other. If you cannot create a good design on paper, you will not be able to do so on screen.

If you are doing your own layout, you need to decide on one or two important factors before you put pen to paper, and to bear them in mind as your layout develops:

- The perception of your audience

- The AIDA principle.

THE AUDIENCE'S PERCEPTION

How do you want the readers to see you? This is the practical application of the image you considered in chapter 4. It is quite separate from the benefits of your product, which you will be putting across in your copy. It is concerned with the impression the readers have of you or your company, or the 'feeling' your product generates.

Look again at the ad in Fig. 7. The image the shop wanted to project was one of youth, vigour, clothes for the modern woman; also of elegance and style. How did they convey that image? They used a young model, but that was not all. Her stance, her expression, the illustration of her in motion, all give the impression of a young woman 'on the move', going places, self-assured, stylish. The clothes are there to help create the image, rather than being the subject of the ad. It is also uncluttered, with a lot of white space, giving an impression of leisured elegance, definitely up-market.

Techniques for creating an image

There are a number of techniques for influencing your audience's perception. Here are a few:

- Using 'atmospheric' illustrations. For example, a 'woodcut' type line drawing gives an impression of traditional charm, even though it may have no direct relevance to the product. In the same way an obviously foreign scene may give an exotic look. And as we saw with the ad in Fig. 7 the way the model is photographed can itself convey an image.

- The way the product is illustrated. A soft-focus photograph implies romance; a simple, sharp picture can look modern.

- Specific references in the copy. The image can be built up by telling people how you perceive yourself, and by the use of key words which position you. For example, 'natural' and 'wholesome' imply goodness when applied to food; 'elegant' probably means that your product is good by expensive.

- The style in which the copy is written. For example, an ad written as though it comes personally from the proprietor, with lots of approving references to the staff, can give an impression of a friendly family concern.

- The way the ad is laid out. A very 'busy' ad, for example, with a lot in it, and plenty of price or saving flashes, has a 'cheap and cheerful' look; it says quite clearly, 'Come to us if bargains are what you want!' The ad in Fig. 8 is a good example of this approach. There is plenty going on, without the reader getting lost, and the overall effect is of a lot of bargains. The ad in Fig. 7, by contrast, is laid out in an uncluttered, elegant way – rather like a fashion shop window in fact.

Most images, of course, are created by using a combination of techniques, and you will no doubt find others. Whatever technique you use, it is important to bear in mind throughout the design stage how you want the readers to perceive you.

What are you advertising?

This may seem a silly question, but many people do lose sight of what it is they need to get across to the public. Normally it is *not* your company that you are promoting. In most cases it is not even the product. It is usually the **benefits** of the product. That is what people want to know about.

Many advertisers make the mistake of putting their name, or that of their company, instead of a headline, sometimes even with a photograph of themselves in the most prominent part of the ad. Why should the public care what you look like? Why should they want to know your name before anything else? They will probably need the name of your company eventually, but only after they have been persuaded by the benefits of your product.

Write for the reader

Forgetting the reader is so easily done. I was once commissioned to write copy for a brochure for a small local company. I wrote an eye-catching headline for the front cover, which I felt captured the company's image and invited one to look inside. Later, the designer who had commissioned me said how pleased the client had been with my copy. 'He only made one change,' he said. He showed me the finished brochure. The eye-catching headline was banished to the back, and in its place on the front cover was the name, address and telephone number of the company. Just one change, but completely counter-productive. What that client forgot was one of the golden rules of advertising:

- Always look at your ad *from the point of view of the reader.*

The reader needed to know the name and address of the advertiser, but only *after* he had been convinced that he needed the service being offered.

Fig. 8. A good 'busy' ad can leave the impression that you have a lot of bargains to offer.

MAGNIFICENT DRIVEWAYS,

MODEST PRICES.

Nothing, absolutely nothing compares with a Town & Country Driveway. Although it's beautiful to look at and modestly priced, its beauty is more than skin deep. Beneath the surface is a unique fibre reinforcement that prevents sinking and spreading. It's surface, once sealed, is over 25% harder than the surface of concrete. It's completely weed and maintenance free. Available in a range of finishes and stunning natural colours. THE TOWN & COUNTRY SERVICE, starts with our free, no obligation site survey and design service. Our skilled installation personnel take care of everything from start to finish in days rather than weeks. The result is a magnificent driveway that's fully guaranteed, and will look and stay beautiful for many years to come. Just phone us now for our free colour brochure or no obligation site survey.

CALL FREE NOW • LINES OPEN 24 HOURS
0800 555660
Alternatively Freepost the coupon today.

Town & Country Driveways, FREEPOST, Manchester M22 5GJ.
Please arrange for my free site survey ☐ Please send me my free brochure of Town & Country driveways ☐

Name _____

Telephone _____

Address _____

GW 4/95

Town & Country Driveways
Tougher than they have to be.
TOWN & COUNTRY DRIVEWAYS, SHARSTON HOUSE, SHARSTON ROAD, MANCHESTER.

Fig. 9. The AIDA principle in action. First the ad attracts the attention; then it stimulates interest; then it creates a desire for the product. Finally it invites action.

THE AIDA PRINCIPLE

There is a long-established mnemonic in selling, which is particularly relevant in advertising. It is called AIDA:

- First attract **attention.**

- Then stimulate **interest**.

- Next create a **desire.**

- Finally invite **action.**

Attention
Your headline, sometimes in combination with the main illustration, should attract attention – stop your readers turning the page.

Interest
The subheading, illustrations or first sentence or two should capture their interest, and make them want to look further.

Desire
The main body of the copy, together with any other illustrations, should be aimed at pointing out the benefits of the product or service, and making the reader desire it.

Action
Finally, you need to tell people how to get hold of your product – invite action. If yours is a direct response ad, then it is the coupon that does it, together with an exhortation, perhaps, along the lines of 'Don't delay, post this coupon *today*.' If there is no coupon, the 'action' part of the ad can be 'Give us a ring *now!*' or 'Visit your local tackle shop.'

The action you are inviting can also be something more passive. It can simply be for people to think favourably of the product, so that they ask for it next time they are shopping. This type of 'invitation to action' can be the company's slogan, or a final sentence or two in the body copy either summarising the product's benefits or pointing out new ones.

The principle in action
A very good example of the AIDA principle is shown in the ad in Fig. 9. The headline with its juxtaposition of 'magnificent driveways' and 'modest prices', attracts the **attention. Interest** is stimulated by the reinforcement of this message in the first couple of sentences, and in the

detail that follows. The **desire** is created by the reference to the fact that the driveway is guaranteed and will look beautiful for many years. And the **action** is clear: phone now for a free colour brochure, with the telephone number shown clearly.

This principle can be applied to almost any medium. The one exception is the outdoor poster. As most people see posters 'on the move', very often from their cars, you don't have time for long messages, and a slogan and an illustration are usually all you can effectively use.

The AIDA principle in brochures

Brochures work on the same principle, although there you have rather more space to work with. The front cover is the **attention**-grabber, and it is important that its message should encourage people to look inside.

It therefore serves a dual function of attracting attention and stimulating **interest**. Since the reader cannot see the whole thing in one glance, as he can with a space ad, it is important that the front cover should indicate what is on offer. This means that clever but slightly obscure headlines, always a bit tricky, are definitely out for this medium. An illustration is useful on the front cover.

Inside the brochure is where you do the selling, creating the **desire** for your product. Having a lot of space can create its own problems, as you need to keep the interest going with more headlines, illustrations and cross-heads (subheadings which break up the text). The trick is in variety – different-sized illustrations, copy broken up, different typefaces perhaps.

Finally, the back is concerned with the **action**. This is where you should put instructions on how to order, where to go to buy the product, together with the coupon if there is one, and your logo and slogan.

THE ELEMENTS OF THE AD

Before we move on to the elements which will make up your layout, think what your *readers* will look at first, and therefore what is most important to them. Experts have found that people look at the various elements in this order:

- Headline and main illustration

- Other large illustrations and captions

- Cross-heads or other eye-catching devices

- Any small drawings which break up the text

- Body copy.

Five times as many people read the headline as read the body copy – a sobering thought! Even professional advertisers can only retain the interest of one person in five throughout the ad. Don't make the mistake of thinking that the body copy doesn't matter, however. It would be tragic if, having retained the interest of that one reader in five all through the rest of the ad, you lost him at the end through poor copy!

Headlines

At this stage, it is not necessary to know exactly what words you will choose for your headline. But it is important to have a good general idea, so that you know approximately how much space to allow for in your layout. This is not as difficult as it may seem. Look at your list of benefits; the most important one is likely to form the basis for your headline. If there are two benefits you want to emphasise, and they will go together neatly, then the headline is likely to be longer.

Example
A hardware store has as its USP the fact that it offers a wider range of tools than anyone else in the area. This benefit can be expressed fairly succinctly. The headline is likely to be something along the lines of

The Widest Range of Tools in Town

Whether these are the actual words used in the final headline, or whether in the writing it gets changed to something like

Why the Experts Buy Their Tools from Us

you know that it is going to use up about seven or eight words. You don't have to be precise, because there is a degree of flexibility in the design. If the headline is a little shorter than you have allowed for, it can 'float' quite happily in a bit of extra white space. If it is a little longer, a slightly more condensed typeface or a slight reduction in the type size will solve the problem.

Occasionally, of course, you will change your mind about a headline as you are writing it, and it will be far too long. A health food shop may have as its USP that all its food is natural and wholesome. You would then assume that the headline would be along the lines of

Only Natural Ingredients Used

even though you might want to polish it up, and make it more snappy. When you actually start writing, however, you may come up with something a little more eye-catching like

Less Fat, Less Sugar, Less Salt, Less Everything
– Except Goodness

You wouldn't be able to squeeze this into the space allowed for the first headline. In that case, you would have to revise your layout.

Then why not write the headline before doing the layout? If that suits you best, by all means do it that way.

There are two reasons why many people do the layout first.

- The headline is a vital part of an ad but there is a danger that, if you write it first, you will end up designing the ad around the headline. The concept of the ad needs to be looked at as a whole, with each element playing its correct part. Unless the headline you write is absolutely brilliant, your ad will lose impact if the other elements are secondary to it.

- You may need to consult partners or colleagues about the ad, and if they don't like the layout you could have wasted a lot of time on the headline to no avail.

Having said that, there are people who write the headline first, and do so very successfully. Be flexible. If you do come up with a really good headline that is a bit longer than you allowed for, be prepared to tinker with the layout – it will seldom need more than that.

Other eye-catching devices

The headline is the main device for attracting attention, but you ought to be aware of others, so that you can incorporate them in your design if they are appropriate. The most common are:

- bullet points
- flashes.

Bullet points are a series of short statements or items in list form, usually preceded by a black dot, as with the words 'bullet points' and 'flashes' above. In advertising they are used for highlighting benefits or information of some sort – the subjects covered by a book, for

Fig. 10. Sample flashes which can emphasise points in an ad.

example, a list of services offered by a garage, the facilities available at a hotel – even a complete list of the benefits your product offers. We will see how to write them in chapter 6, but for now you just need to decide whether they will be part of your layout, and how much space will be needed for them. Sometimes they can form part of the body copy, in which case you do not have to allow space especially for them, but often they need to be treated as an element of the ad in their own right.

Flashes come in all kinds of shapes. There are ovals, circles, starbursts, rectangles, diamonds and many others. Fig. 10 shows some of the many types available. They are often used to show prices or savings, but can be used to highlight a second major benefit which is not included in the headline. They often overlap an illustration, particularly if what they contain relates to the product illustrated. They have even been used for filling a blank space in the design! You should always know what you are going to say in a flash, however, before you put it in your layout. It can be extremely frustrating, at copywriting stage, to sit racking your brains to think of something to put into a flash that was included at layout stage just because it looked good!

A corner flash is often used across a corner of an ad for a sort of 'stop press' item – 'Just open', for example, or 'New design'.

Illustrations
Illustrations provide variety in an ad, but they are not essential. The main reasons for using illustrations are to:

• show the product

• provide atmosphere

• demonstrate the product in action

• make people interested in the ad and get them reading

• break up the text.

Now is the time to decide what kind of pictures you are going to use, what they are going to illustrate and their size and shape. There are any number of different kinds of illustration, but there are two main categories.

Photographs
Photos are the most common form of illustration in advertising. People are used to looking at photographs, and generally believe them.

According to the old adage, the camera never lies. Photographs are usually easy to obtain, and they can show scale.

Line drawings
Line drawings (straightforward black and white drawings using only black lines) and **line and tone** illustrations (which use shading) can, however, be better in certain circumstances:

- On **poor paper**, when the ink on photographs is likely to run, blurring the illustration.

- For **atmosphere**, where they can create an idealised world which can't be captured in a photograph.

- To show **detail**. A photograph, particularly in a small ad or on poor paper, may not show the style and cut of a coat clearly enough, whereas a slightly stylised line drawing will.

- To show a **cutaway** picture, such as the inside of a car.

- For **technical** illustrations.

If your ad is in colour, then your line drawing too can be in colour. It should still be drawn in black and white; you specify the colours you want with the artwork.

Size and shape of illustrations

Having decided whether you want photographs, line drawings or a combination, you need to consider their size and shape. Variety creates interest, so if you are using more than one illustration, vary their size and position on the layout.

You can also have photographs **cutting into** each other (giving the effect of one slightly overlapping the other), or you can use a **cut-out**, in which the background is cut away, leaving just the object or person you want to illustrate. This is useful for showing someone modelling clothes, for example, where the background is irrelevant. It can also be used if there is something in the background which is likely to distract the reader from the main object. The techniques for cut-outs is described in chapter 8.

Obtaining illustrations

Having decided on the size, shape and type of illustrations you would like, you have to get hold of them. If your ad contains some general illustrations – two people running across a meadow, a tropical island, an animal study, etc – you can obtain them from a **picture library**. For advice on finding and dealing with picture libraries, see chapter 9.

If you want line drawings of general subjects, you will find that there are several **instant art** books available which contain drawings of a wide range of subjects, all ready for you to copy or to transfer onto your artwork. You are unlikely to find these books in any except the largest bookshops, but a good art shop should be able to help you. They are expensive, but they contain drawings of almost any subject imaginable. And if you have a DTP system, you may find a selection of images on your system or available to purchase on disk or CD.

If the illustrations you want are specific to your advertisement – shots of a product, scenes in a hotel, etc – then you will either need to commission them or draw or photograph them yourself.

Using photographs
Unless you are an experienced photographer, I would not recommend trying to do your own advertising photography. Because of the way ads are reproduced, the photographs must be of a very high standard, both in terms of composition and in terms of clarity. 'Holiday snap' type pictures never reproduce well, and will make your ad look shoddy. You will therefore need to commission a photographer. See chapter 9 for more on dealing with professional photographers.

Using line drawings
If you are good at drawing, you may be able to do your own line drawings. If you decide to try it, be sure to use clean, good-quality paper and a black pen, and that your work is clean and clear. Any smudges or marks will show. Avoid too many lines close together, especially if your ad is to be reproduced on poor paper, as they tend to blur. If you make a small mistake, correcting fluid will usually cover it without showing when the artwork is printed.

If you are not artistic, you will have to commission someone to do your line drawings. See chapter 9 for advice on how to hire an illustrator. Some designers can do line drawings, but be careful. The fact that someone is a good designer does not necessarily mean they can draw, so don't automatically assume that a designer will be able to do your line drawings.

What kind of illustrations, and how many?
The following questionnaire should help you clarify your ideas on what illustrations you need, if any, and whether they should be photographs or line illustrations.

How we understand private banking

Commitment
In 1898, we valued private clients. We still do.

Quality
Private banking relationships involving £150,000 and more
demand high quality service. Quality is the hallmark of the Swiss.

Expertise
Investment expertise should not be limited to the UK. We also
take a global view.

Security
Security and financial strength should be beyond question. Our
Triple 'A' rating places us in a very select club.

Personal Service
Each private client should expect an individual customer advisor.
Yours is waiting to meet you.

If you like our view of private banking, why not call either
Martyn Folland in London on 01-606 4000,
Mark Deeble-Rogers in Manchester on 061-834 2448, or
Alan Stewart in Edinburgh on 031-225 9186.
Or complete and return the coupon below.

To: Martyn Folland, Swiss Bank Corporation, 30A Charles II Street,
London SW1Y 4AE.

Please provide me with details of your private banking services. ☐

Please contact me by telephone to arrange a meeting. ☐

Name (Mr/Mrs/Miss) _____

Address _____

_____

_____

Postcode _____ Telephone _____ GM/1

A member of IMRO

**Swiss Bank
Corporation**
in the UK

Now also in Jersey at 40 Esplanade, St. Helier. Tel: (0534) 36341.

Fig. 11. An unillustrated ad which manages to look interesting
without the aid of pictures.

84

1. Is the product capable of being illustrated?

2. If so, would it benefit from being shown in action?

3. Would an illustration help provide atmosphere and create the right image?

4. Could the atmosphere or image best be created with a photograph or a line illustration?

5. Should the product be illustrated with a line drawing, in order to show detail or technical specifications?

6. Would the ad benefit from a combination of photographs and line drawings?

7. Could line drawings be used as a frame for the main body of the ad?

If you have to compromise between the number of pictures you would like and the number that will fit comfortably into the space you have, don't choose a lot of illustrations and show them all postage-stamp size. It is much better to cut the number of pictures, and show them large enough to make an impact.

Presenting illustrations to the printer

Whether you are commissioning illustrations or doing your own, it is important to know the form in which they will need to be presented to the publication or the printer. They will usually tell you if they have any special requirements, but generally speaking colour photographs should be in the form of transparencies or colour prints, and black and white photographs in the form of prints. Don't send negatives to the printer. If you are using a colour photograph in a black and white ad, make sure that there is enough contrast, so that it is clear. Photographs which look good in colour don't always look so good when reproduced in black and white if there are too many dark or light shades.

Line illustrations should be drawn on a sheet of clean white paper, preferably to the right size, so that they can be pasted straight on to the artwork when that stage is reached.

Captions can be important if the pictures need explaining, but don't include them if they merely repeat what is obvious from the illustrations themselves.

Times Bold – abcdefghijklmnopqrstuvwxyz
ABCDEFGHIJKLMNOPQRSTUVWXYZ

Times Italic – *abcdefghijklmnopqrstuvwxyz*
ABCDEFGHIJKLMNOPQRSTUVWXYZ

Helvetica Medium – abcdefghijklmnopqrstuvwxyz
ABCDEFGHIJKLMNOPQRSTUVWXYZ

Helvetica Bold – **abcdefghijklmnopqrstuvwxyz**
ABCDEFGHIJKLMNOPQRSTUVWXYZ

Zapf Chancery Book – *abcdefghijklmnopqrstuvwxyz*
ABCDEFGHIJKLMNOPQRSTUVWXYZ

Plantin – abcdefghijklmnopqrstuvwxyz
ABCDEFGHIJKLMNOPQRSTUVWXYZ

Plantin Bold – **abcdefghijklmnopqrstuvwxyz**
ABCDEFGHIJKLMNOPQRSTUVWXYZ

Palatino – abcdefghijklmnopqrstuvwxyz
ABCDEFGHIJKLMNOPQRSTUVWXYZ

Palatino Italics – *abcdefghijklmnopqrstuvwxyz*
ABCDEFGHIJKLMNOPQRSTUVWXYZ

Rockwell Light – abcdefghijklmnopqrstuvwxyz
ABCDEFGHIJKLMNOPQRSTUVWXYZ

Souvenir Demi – **abcdefghijklmnopqrstuvwxyz**
ABCDEFGHIJKLMNOPQRSTUVWXYZ

Univers Extra Bold – **abcdefghijklmnopqrstuvwxyz**
ABCDEFGHIJKLMNOPQRSTUVWXYZ

Baskerville – abcdefghijklmnopqrstuvwxyz
ABCDEFGHIJKLMNOPQRSTUVWXYZ

Fig. 12. The use of different typefaces, such as these, can create almost any 'look' or image which you require.

Body copy

Body copy is the actual text of the ad. You don't need to know at this stage just *what* you are going to say in your body copy, but you do need to know approximately *how much* you are going to say, in order to allocate the right amount of space. It is also useful to know whether your copy will divide into separate 'blocks'. If it will, you can use each block as a separate element in your layout, giving you a wider choice of possible designs.

If your ad is going to be all type, without any illustrations at all, you will need to work harder to make it look interesting. There are several ways in which this can be done; by:

- imaginative use of headlines, eg using more than one, or putting the headline in an interesting position

- using a clear and interesting typeface

- using a variety of typefaces

- using cross-heads

- *using* the layout, eg having the copy typeset in an interesting shape. If you do this, make sure that it is a simple shape with straight edges, and that the shape does not make the copy too hard to read.

You will discover other techniques for yourself. Look carefully at other people's unillustrated advertisements, and see what you can learn from them. If you look at the ad in Fig. 11 you will see just how eye-catching and interesting a copy-only ad can look. It uses a bold headline, simple cross-heads and a clear typeface; the layout is uncluttered and interesting. Another good example is the B & G ad on page 106. The main message with an unillustrated ad, therefore, is to make it look interesting, and avoid a boring-looking mass of text.

Typefaces

A **typeface** is a particular design of lettering. The text of this book, for example, is set in Times, while the headings are in Helvetica Bold. You can see that they both have a very distinctive 'look'. Page 86 shows a few of the many typefaces available. Decide what kind of typeface or faces you are going to use in your ad at this stage, and also what **type size**. If you look at passages of text in different typefaces, you will find that the number of characters (letters, punctuation marks or symbols) in a given area of text varies considerably. Before writing your copy, therefore, you should be able to estimate how many words you need to write.

There are thousands of different typefaces, and whole books have been written on the subject of typography, but for most purposes you only need to know the basics.

The most common typefaces have **serifs**, little cross-lines which finish off the letters – like the letters in the main text of this book. Typefaces which do not have serifs are called **sans serif** – like the letters in the headings. Most people find serifed typefaces easier to read in large blocks than sans serif, but the latter can look quite stylish and modern, and is perfectly legible if well spaced. Consult your typesetter if you plan to use one, or look at the typefaces on your DTP system to decide what is right for you, bearing in mind the image you are trying to convey, the type of ad and the number of typefaces you are using. Obviously some typefaces go better together than others, but don't use too many different ones, as the ad will begin to look untidy, and will lose its unity. It is seldom necessary to use more than two. For advice on contacting and dealing with typesetters, see chapter 9.

Type sizes

The unit of measurement of type sizes is the **point**, and the most common type size for body copy is 9 or 10 point. You can, however, use whatever size you think is right for your ad.

Leading

One final point to consider is **leading**. Absence of spacing between lines (solid type) can sometimes make text difficult to read, particularly if there is a lot of it and if the typeface is condensed. You can therefore introduce leading – extra spacing between lines. Type which is specified as 10/11, for example, will be set in 10 point, with one point of space between the lines. This makes the copy easier to read. (There are 72 points in an inch.)

Copy length

Once you have decided on your typeface and size, you can estimate how much copy to write. You can use your typesetter's type book and count the number of characters in a given line length or area, or simply type a passage on your DTP system using your preferred type.

Using logos and slogans

A **logo** is an emblem or device by which a product or company can easily be recognised – the stylised bird on Bird's Eye products, for example, or the distinctive lettering of Boots. It can be very useful in creating an immediate association with the product in the public's mind, and should be used on letterheads, company vans and buildings as well as in ads. It is not necessary to have anything elaborate designed. Just your name in a distinctive typeface is sufficient, if used consistently.

Whether you have a logo or not, your company name, or the name of your product, should appear on your ad, and the best place for it is the bottom right-hand corner. This is the final 'sign-off' and it is important that you leave the reader with something positive. That is why many logos either incorporate a slogan, or are accompanied by one.

A **slogan** should preferably tell the reader something about your *company*, and is therefore different from the headline which attracts attention to the *benefits of the product*. A dress shop, for example, might advertise a range of its products under the headline

High Fashion at Low Prices

That tells the reader something about the products – their benefits. It might sign off something like

Anytown Fashions
Service with a smile

That tells you something about the company, or the image desired.

The slogan should leave the reader feeling good about the company. It should also be used regularly, not changed with each ad, as it is by repeating the slogan that the image is conveyed. Look at the ad in Fig. 19. At the bottom is Birkbeck's slogan, 'Access and excellence'. This is a good example of the principle behind slogans. It leaves the reader with a positive impression of the college.

DESIGNING THE LAYOUT

Proportion and unity

When designing your ad, try putting the various elements in different positions to see which looks best. No book can tell you what is going to look right for any particular ad – that is where your creativity comes in! Decide on the relative sizes of each element; make sure that they are in proportion – that your headline does not overpower the illustration, or that the body copy doesn't squeeze out the main picture.

The various elements of the ad must come together to make a harmonious whole, not a lot of separate items. So don't spoil it with too many typefaces, and don't split it up too much. It should have variety, but also be balanced visually, allowing the eye to travel through the ad in a logical fashion.

Fig. 13. Thumbnail sketches – the first step in designing an ad.

 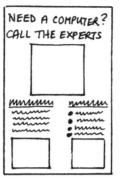 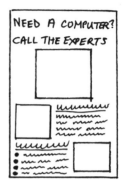

Larger sketches of the most promising layouts.

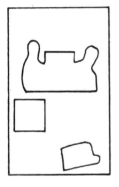 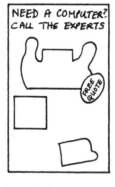 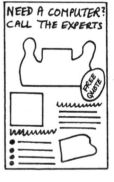

1. Draw in the outlines of illustrations.

2. Put in the headline and other eye-catching devices

3. Insert lines for the body copy.

Fig. 14. Stages in the final layout.

White space

Don't be afraid of **white space**. Don't think that you must fill the whole ad with text or illustration. As you can see from many of the ads shown in this book, white space can actually be as much an element in the design as copy or pictures, and it needs to be considered in the same light. Look again at the ad in Fig. 7. At a casual glance, it may seem as though the white space is unimportant – it is just where the designer didn't put anything. But try to imagine that space filled. The ad would lose much of its impact – it would look less elegant.

Rough sketches

If you have a DTP system you can play around with various layouts, putting your illustrations, headlines and copy in different positions, and then changing them if they don't look right. But if you don't have such a system, the best way to get your layout right is first to do a number of **thumbnail sketches** – small rough drawings showing the various elements in different positions. Fig. 13 shows a few such sketches for an ad with a headline, one big and two smaller photographs and body copy to cover about one-third of the area. As you can see, they are very rough and very small, and they don't have to be at all accurate. But they give a reasonable idea of the general 'look' of that particular design.

From those thumbnail sketches, choose the two or three you like best, and do those rather larger, with more detail – the headline can now consist of words, the positions of the illustrations can be shown more accurately, cross-heads, bullet points, etc can be indicated (see Fig. 14).

The final layout

Choose from those two or three the one that now looks best, and draw that one accurately to the correct size and shape. The sketches in Fig. 14 show the stages you need to follow.

- First, rule lines to denote the outlines of any photographs, making sure that they are also the right size and shape, and that their position and angle is right.

- Indicate the position of any line drawings by a rough sketch, or by drawing outlines as for the photographs.

- Get the outline of a line drawing or a cut-out photograph right, do not just draw a square where it is to go, as text may have to go into the 'cut away' part. Even if it doesn't, you won't get a reliable impression of the final ad unless you show the layout as accurately as possible. An accurate layout will also provide a guide for your photographer or illustrator.

- Mark on the layout which pictures are to go where, to avoid confusion later.

- Put the headline in. Draw it in with a felt pen; it is best to use actual words, even if they are not the ones you have finally chosen.

- Finally put in lines to indicate where the body copy is to go, and any other devices such as flashes or bullet points.

Avoid the temptation to run copy round awkwardly-shaped illustrations. It may look good on your layout, and it can be effective when done professionally. But it is almost impossible for the amateur to get right. It is best to stick to straight lines.

If you have estimated your copy lengths, illustration sizes, etc correctly, it should all fit in. Even professional designers get it wrong sometimes, however, so you might find that the space left for copy is not big enough for the number of words you wanted to write. You will then either need to write less copy, or cut down on the number of illustrations. If you decide that you can do with less copy, you can keep the same layout, but if you need to drop an illustration, it will usually mean redrawing the layout.

Even when using a DTP system, it is often a good idea to do (and perhaps even print out) a rough layout before finalising the copy and illustrations. In that way you can be sure that the overall effect is right before becoming involved in the detail.

When you have done your layout, and are satisfied with it, put it aside. Leave it overnight, and look at it again the next morning. If it still looks good, it is probably going to make a good ad.

CASE STUDIES

Peter's ads are simple

Peter Jackson's ads are very simple to lay out; they are small and he doesn't need to illustrate anything. All he needs to worry about is that he includes all his benefits, and that the ads follow the AIDA principle. He therefore starts with a headline – not his name, as many others do, but a headline, so that his ads stand out a bit more. He sketches out roughly what they will look like. He doesn't need to be too exact, because there are no illustrations and no real design element.

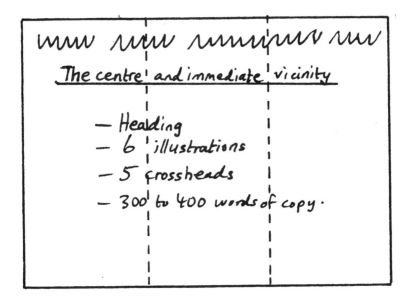

Inside.

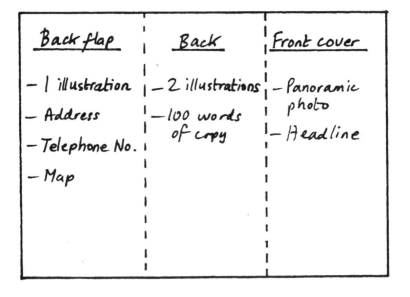

Outside.

Fig. 15. The Talbots' plan for the roll-fold brochure.

John and Sylvia enlist a designer

Neither John nor Sylvia Talbot is particularly creative, so although they are happy to do their small ads themselves, they decide to spend some of their advertising budget on getting a designer to do the layout and the artwork for their brochure. The designer will charge them £300 for the whole job, and they will have to pay another £250 or so for a photographer to take the ten shots they need.

Although they are not doing the layout themselves, they spend quite a lot of time briefing the designer on what they want. The layout of a roll-fold brochure needs careful attention. Although it has many advantages it does not 'follow through' from front to back in the way that a normal brochure does. There are two 'sides' and this has to be taken into account.

What they decide on is a panoramic photograph of the area for the front cover, with a brief 'headline' overprinted on it. The inside is to be treated as one big spread, with a headline across the whole length, several cross-heads and six illustrations. This section will cover the centre itself, but will also include some shots of the horses out on the rides, and information on the immediate vicinity. The back flap will show another photograph, and will contain details of the address and telephone number of the centre and how to get there. The remaining panel, which forms the 'back' of the brochure, will be devoted to a description, with two photographs, of the general area. So the general organisation will be as shown in Fig. 15.

Mary does her own layout

Mary Davies decides to do her own layout, as hers are simple ads, and she has a certain amount of imagination. She doesn't need to say a lot about her shop, so most of the copy will be in bullet point form, and there will be quite a lot of white space – which she feels she needs to convey the idea that the shop is spacious and pleasant to browse around. She will pay a professional photographer £25 a time to photograph a collection of books for each of the three big ads she has planned.

She decides on a standard format for all three ads, so that an identity is established. Her final layout is shown in Fig. 16.

The video makers do their own photography

Like Mary Davies, Vidco also decide to do their own layout. Between them, the partners feel they have enough creativity to do a good job. One of the partners is a good photographer, and photographing the videos in their cases is relatively simple, so they will also do their own photography. The illustration of an 'improved' golfer they can get as a still from one of their videos. They want to say quite a lot, and they

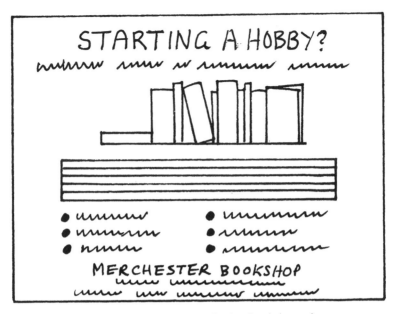

Fig. 16. Mary Davies' plan for her bookshop ad.

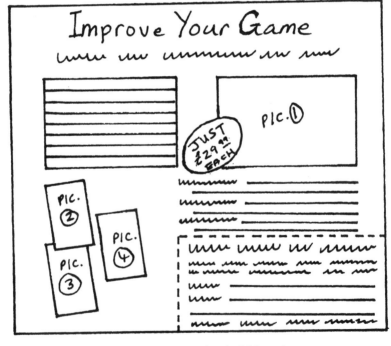

Fig 17. The layout for the Vidco ad.

need a coupon, so their ad is going to be quite full. Their layout is shown in Fig 17.

CHECKLIST

- Can you do the layout yourself, or will you have to hire a designer?

- If you are doing your own layout, how do you plan to project your image?

- Are you advertising your product's benefits, or just yourself?

- Do your ideas for your ad follow the logical progression of the AIDA principle?

- How long is your headline likely to be and are you going to use any other devices?

- What pictures are you going to use? How do you plan to get hold of them?

- How much space will you need for body copy, and can it be broken up?

- What typefaces and sizes will you use?

- Are you going to incorporate a logo and a slogan?

- Have you tried out various designs?

- Are you still happy with your final layout, having left it overnight?

6
Headlines and Other Devices

The average reader spends just one and a half seconds looking at an ad. That is how long you have to stimulate their interest and make them read further; you won't do it by putting your name and address in the most prominent position! A punchy eye-catching headline is essential, and many copywriters spend more time on getting that right than they do on the rest of the copy.

If you feel you can't write your own headline and body copy, there are **freelance copywriters**. See chapter 9 for advice on finding and dealing with them.

The headline will usually proclaim your product's main benefits, but you need to give a lot of thought to how you express it. When you have considered it for some time, try writing a headline. Put it aside, perhaps overnight, and then look at it again. How does it sound now? Can it be improved with a bit of polishing? Will one or two word changes make it read better? Or does the whole idea look wrong? Make any changes you think are necessary, then leave it again and look at it a third time.

If despite all your efforts, the right headline doesn't come, forget about it. Write the rest of the ad and come back to it. As you write the body copy you could find that a sentence or phrase stands out which would make a good headline.

Before we examine the different kinds of headline, and a few other devices, here are a few general tips on headline writing.

- Be specific. If you are offering a fifty per cent reduction on all stock, say 50% Off All Stock, not Amazing Offer.

- If your product is aimed at a particular group of people, put a word in the headline to identify them: Calling All Cat-Lovers!

- Don't be afraid to use prices or figures in your headline, but only do so if they will contribute to the main aim of attracting attention. A Weekend in Paris for Only £59.

- You can combine two benefits in one headline, but only if they go together and can be expressed concisely.

- Keep it simple. Avoid scientific terms in a headline – unless of course it is aimed at scientists.

- Avoid puns or other trick headlines. If the audience doesn't have your sense of humour, puns can be counter-productive. The big agencies sometimes use them, but they have the budgets to give them constant exposure – even then they sometimes backfire.

- Avoid unnecessary adjectives, like amazing or exciting. They lengthen the headline, making it less punchy, and few people believe them. If something really *is* exciting, say so in the copy, and better still say why, and sell the benefit.

- Avoid long words, and be colloquial without being slangy.

- Headlines should *complement* the illustrations, not repeat in words what they say visually.

CHOOSING THE RIGHT STYLE

Creating statement headlines

These are the most straightforward headlines of all: they simply make a statement about what you are selling. Because of their simplicity, they can often be very effective. Readers immediately know what you are selling, or what it is going to do for them, and if they are interested they will read further. They work particularly well when there is a price or a saving included. The typical book club offer of 3 Books for Just £1.50 and the retailer's ad which says Up to 50% Off All Stock are both effective examples of this kind of headline. People are attracted to the idea of savings or cheap offers, and that kind of headline catches their attention.

You can also introduce a slight twist into a statement headline, to make the readers take a second look. For example, an advertisement for a pocket guidebook might have the headline:

The Cotswolds in Your Pocket

This looks slightly incongruous, and definitely intriguing. It makes the reader wonder what you mean, and look at the ad more carefully to find out.

Fig. 18. An ad whose headline makes a generalised comparison.

Creating comparison headlines

A variation on the statement headline is the comparison. If your main benefit is that you are better than the competition in some way, why not say so? A comparison between yourself and the rest can be effective. The ad in Fig. 18 is a good example of a generalised comparison. The double headline implies that other pumps are either unreliable or unaffordable, without actually saying so. This is often the best kind of comparison to make. If the advertisers had said that they offered cheaper, more reliable pumps than anyone else, they would have fallen foul of the British Code of Advertising Practice unless they could prove that no other pump was cheaper and more reliable. By generalising in this way, the implication is there without the need for proof.

You can be more specific, but specific comparisons can bring certain problems, apart from the possible conflict with BCAP mentioned above. You could say something like:

We Stock a Wider Range of Power Tools than Bloggs Hardware

if that is true. But such a headline might sting Bloggs into retaliating. If he wrote a series of ads headed

We Give Better Service than Smiths Tools and We Offer Credit

you could find yourself locked into a rather silly tit-for-tat battle which could end up putting the customers off both shops.

Creating invitation headlines

This is a fairly common form of headline, which involves the reader, suggesting that he or she try something or do something. It is a different way of making a statement about your product. Instead of saying

Our Hotel is in Beautiful Devon

you could express it as

Come and Join Us in Beautiful Devon.

If your product does something for people, it is very easy – and very effective – to make the changes. Instead of

Primrose Shampoo Puts Body in Your Hair

say

Put Body in Your Hair
with Primrose Shampoo

That makes it more positive. It also involves your audience, and makes them feel as though you are addressing them personally.

BIRKBECK COLLEGE
UNIVERSITY OF LONDON

Are you bored at work?

Do you want more from your job?

Are you interested in global issues?

Do you care about the environment?

Studying Geography at Birkbeck you can develop new skills and confidence and enhance your career prospects

◆ team-building ◆ presentation skills
◆ research techniques ◆ project writing
◆ information technology and GIS
◆ field trips in the UK and Europe

whilst studying world economic, environmental and social problems. Get a *BA/BSc Geography* degree in only 4 years by part-time evening study. The Geography Department is conveniently located within minutes of Tottenham Court Road tube station.

Normal entry qualifications may not apply if you are over 21. Payment of fees can be spread over 8 months.

For more information contact:
Merle Abbott, Department of Geography, Birkbeck College, 7 - 15 Gresse Street, London W1P 2LL or call 0171 631 6471, giving the reference GE1.

ACCESS AND EXCELLENCE

Fig. 19. A good example of using questions in a headline.

Combined with an illustration, this kind if headline can be used as a sort of 'see yourself in this situation' ad. A travel company ad showing a picture of someone lying on a tropical beach, with a headline

Fly with Us to Paradise

sets off all sorts of daydreams in the reader's mind. On a less ambitious scale, a bath salts ad could show someone relaxing in a fragrant bath with a headline

Treat Yourself to a Touch of Luxury Tonight.

Creating question headlines

Another way of attracting readers' attention is to put your headline in the form of a question. If the question is the right one, it can strike a chord with just the people you are trying to reach. Question headlines very often work well with a response in the form of a subheading. A florist, for example, might have a poster in a hotel used by business travellers, saying

Missing Your Wife?
Send Her Some Flowers

Question headlines can also be used on their own, with the body copy providing the response. A loan company could say simply

Need a Loan?

and then go straight into the main text, explaining how they can help.

You can make your question headline as short and to the point as this, or you can extend it by asking other, related, questions. But beware: this only works if the questions are brief and to the point. The ad shown opposite asks four questions, which makes the headline rather long; but they are all pertinent and punchy, so they work well.

Creating 'why' and 'how' headlines

Two variations of the 'question' approach are the 'why' and the 'how' headlines. They make the ad look more interesting than a straightforward statement, and they enable you to follow with a reasoned argument in favour of your product. Instead of saying simply

Top Sportsmen Use the Jones Ankle Support

you can change it to read

Why Do Top Sportsmen Use the Jones Ankle Support?

Similarly you can change

Make Your Money Work for You

to

How Can You Make Your Money Work for You?

This last headline would probably look better as

How to Make Your Money Work for You.

This leads to the second point about 'why' and 'how' headlines. They can be expressed in the form of a question or not, whichever sounds better.

If you are using these headlines, you must follow the same line in the body. In the first instance above, your body copy would give the reasons why top sportsmen used your ankle support, and in the second it would list the things you need to do to make your money work for you.

Creating testimonial headlines

There was once said to have been an ad with the headline

Mr Ferrari Drives a Fiat.

If that is true it must be everyone's dream of a **testimonial** headline! A testimonial is the endorsement of your product by someone, famous or not. You might find it hard to match the Fiat headline, but there are several ways in which you can use testimonials very effectively in your own ads. Before you use a testimonial headline, however, it is important that you understand BCAP's position (see chapter 2).

If you can get someone well known in your field to endorse your product, as Fiat did above, so much the better; but you can still have a form of testimonial headline without that, by generalising the 'endorsement'. A builder's merchant, for example, could say

Where Leading Builders Get Their Supplies.

Or a computer firm might advertise its programs to the home computer user as

The Software the Professionals Use.

In this way, you can give the impression that the experts use your products, or come to your shop, without having to persuade any of those experts actually to endorse the product.

You can very effectively combine a testimonial and a question headline, as the ad on page 106 shows. The question adds interest to the headline, while the body copy shows how widely used B&G systems are. The impact of all those endorsements means that the advertiser has to write very little additional copy.

Creating 'before' and 'after' headlines

If you want to use this form of headline, you really need to know at the layout stage: it usually affects the way you use illustrations, and the design of the whole ad. What these headlines do is tell readers, or more often show them, what your product will do for them. A hairdresser, for example, might show a picture of a woman with a mop of unruly hair, with the headline From This, followed by a picture of the same woman with a beautifully styled coiffure with the headline To This in 30 Minutes.

CASE STUDIES

The video makers

Vidco have one point they want to bring out more than any other, the emotional buying trigger – that their videos can help improve your golf. Their first thought therefore is a simple statement:

> Our Videos Help You Improve Your Game.

That sounds awful, and is longwinded. They try shortening it and making it a 'how' headline:

> How to Improve Your Game.

This is much better, but is still not punchy enough. So they cut it even further, and turn it into an invitation:

> Improve Your Game.

Ironically, this seems too short and abrupt. They then think of combining two benefits to make a slightly longer, but more punchy, headline. So they finally come up with:

> Improve Your Game in the Comfort of Your Home.

The riding centre

The Talbots need four headlines, one for the January/February ads in the equestrian magazines (advertising summer holidays), one for the autumn ads (advertising weekend and other breaks), one for the front cover of their brochure, and one for the inside. For the magazines, they want something a little different from the other holiday ads, which all look rather similar, and something which will get over the fact that although it is a riding centre, there are lots of other things to do. They start with a statement:

> Riding Holidays with a Difference.

Then they realise that they don't have enough room in their design to

Whose Electronics Consistently Make the Headlines?

B&G Appointed as Official Suppliers to Pierre Fehlmann's 'Grand Mistral' Round-the-World Yacht Race 1996-97

1995 MUMM 36 World's 24 boats start with B&G every winner relied on B&G. Corum Watches wins the World's with B&G!

B&G's Systems carried by every Admiral's Cup Winner

B&G Chosen to Equip all of Chay Blyth's BT Challenge Yachts for their 1996/97 Round-the-World Yacht Race

B&G Systems carried by every single WHITBREAD winner!

When it comes to yachts and powerboat electronics, one name consistently makes headlines around the world. **B&G.**

*In Fact, wherever craft take to the sea for competition or pleasure, **B&G** remains the ultimate standard by which all other marine electronics is judged.*

B&G's Race Winning Software Package B&G Tactician Now Available for Hercules 690, 390 & 290 Systems

Call now for information on B&G's Autopilot and Electronic Systems.

Brookes & Gatehouse Ltd,
Premier Way, Abbey Park, Romsey,
Hampshire, SO51 9AQ England.

Tel: +44 01794 518448
Fax: +44 01794 518077

Fig. 20. An example of a testimonial-type ad.

expand on what is different about their holidays, which will leave readers somewhat in suspense. They also come to the conclusion that since they are advertising in riding magazines, they do not have to include the word 'riding' in the headline – readers would expect the ad to be for some sort of riding holiday. They therefore change it to:

A Family Holiday *Everyone* Enjoys.

This reads well, and they decide to use it. Then Sylvia comes up with a final improvement:

How to Have a Family Holiday *Everyone* Enjoys.

This is a bit more eye-catching, and the reader is encouraged to read the ad to find out how to achieve this difficult feat! There is a slight danger that they may put off some of the young riders who are looking for a holiday on their own, but since it is the self-catering area that the Talbots are most keen to expand into, this headline suits their target audience. There is enough room in the design to expand on that by pointing out the advantage of choosing a riding centre with other attractions nearby, ending with an invitation to send for the brochure.

For the autumn ads, the aim is straightforward – they want to encourage people who might otherwise not have thought of it to have riding weekends. It is John who comes up with the straightforward invitation headline:

Come Riding this Weekend.

Simple and effective, they use it as it is.

For the front of their brochure, they want something a bit like a slogan, but which still tells people what they are offering. They consider

A Family Holiday *Everyone* Enjoys

again, but although this works in a riding magazine, it wouldn't work on its own, as there is nothing to indicate that they are offering riding holidays. They try their 'reject' from the magazines:

Riding Holidays with a Difference

and like it. It invites readers to look inside to see what the difference is. Combined with the name of their centre, it becomes:

Happy Valley for
Riding Holidays with a Difference.

Finally, they must think of a headline for the inside of the brochure. For this, they want to cover the riding side, while still plugging at the fact that there is much more on offer. They start by listing the riding-related activities they offer:

Riding, Trekking, Schooling, Jumping, Dressage and More.

This list looks boring, and, as Sylvia says, they will have to split up the copy with cross-heads, so many of the words will probably be repeated in the cross-heads. So they just list the two main categories of activity:

Riding, Trekking and More.

This is better, but the 'and more' sounds wrong. Then John comes up with:

Riding, Trekking... and a Great Deal More.

They both like this. It rolls off the tongue better, the ellipsis (...) implies that there are aspects of riding which have not been listed, and the words 'a great deal' can be taken in two ways – both to mean 'a lot' and to imply that the deal on offer is great.

The plumber

Peter Jackson is not illustrating his ads, and he therefore needs a particularly prominent headline when trying to get people to employ him to instal their central heating. His primary benefit for this aspect of the business is that he guarantees his work. His first attempt at a headline is:

Central Heating Installed and Guaranteed

but this looks a bit ordinary. His second attempt says:

All Installations Guaranteed.

This is slightly punchier, but it is a bit vague. What kind of installations, the readers might ask – and they might not be interested enough in the answer to read further.

Finally, he realises that not only is his guarantee a benefit, it is a benefit that many other installers don't offer. He therefore decides on a comparison headline, and it all slips into place. He ends up with:

Other Central Heating Installers *Say* Their Work is Good.
I *Guarantee* it.

For his local directory ads, his task is different. There he can't afford to have a long headline, as he doesn't have very much space. Moreover, people looking through a local directory are usually looking for someone in a hurry. He therefore decides to concentrate on his speed, and he chooses a question headline which says:

Need a Plumber – *Fast?*

The bookshop

The benefits that Mary Davies wants to emphasise are different in each of the three ads she has planned. For the June ad, she wants to emphasise holidays and holiday reading, with paperback bestsellers to the fore. She therefore starts off with a statement headline:

The Best in Holiday Reading.

Simple and straightforward though it is, it lacks something, and she is not happy with the word 'best', which is one of those unnecessary adjectives which detract from a headline.

She then wonders whether she is right to emphasise the holiday aspect so much, or whether it would be better to try something just involving summer and relaxation. She then comes up with an invitation headline:

Relax This Summer with a Good Book.

She prefers that, but it is still not quite right. She comes to the conclusion that it is because the connection between the ideas of relaxing and the book is not close enough. By slightly rewording it, she makes:

This Summer, Relax with a Good Book.

This sounds right, and the connection between relaxing and reading is clearly made.

For her September ad, she starts with a straightforward statement:

The Widest Range of Hobby Books in the Area.

This says everything that needs to be said. But then she thinks about those people who may be taking up a hobby, and not even considering buying a book on the subject. Could she attract some of them without actually mentioning books initially? She does it with a question headline, followed by a subheading:

Starting a New Hobby?
We have a book on it.

She can then lead into the first sentence of her copy, explaining that she has the widest range of hobby books in the area.

She is so pleased with this idea that for her Christmas ad she decides to use another question headline. This ones comes first time.

Problems with Presents?
A book is always welcome.

She leaves that one overnight, and still likes it the next day, so that is the one she uses.

OTHER EYE-CATCHING DEVICES

Using cross-heads

Cross-heads are subheadings within the text of an ad. They must be punchy, and they must be factual. They serve a different function from headlines, and mini-headlines will not serve as cross-heads.

The main purpose of cross-heads is usually to break up the text into 'manageable' blocks, but they do have other functions. They can serve a design function, making the ad look more interesting. They can also serve to give the reader a quick guide to what you are offering. Headlines are there primarily to attract attention, but cross-heads provide a kind of resumé of the body copy. Simple one- or two-word cross-heads are all that is usually necessary, each summarising the section of body copy which follows it.

Using bullet points

As explained in chapter 5, bullet points are used to present lists of benefits, facilities, contents etc in a short, pithy format, usually with each item preceded by a dot or star. They should usually be set in **bold** type (heavy type like that used for the word 'bold' above), to make them stand out.

Bullet points are very useful for highlighting certain advantages or aspects of a product. Used properly, they can give a concise summary of what you offer, which can complement the body copy, or even be used instead of body copy.

When using bullet points, bear in mind two things:

1. If each point is too long, the advantage of using bullet points is lost, and you might as well be writing ordinary body copy. Cut out any unnecessary words.

2. Use them to *complement* the body copy, not to waste space repeating what the body copy says.

The ad on page 112 is a very good example of how to use bullet points *instead* of copy. Each point is just a few words long: they are big and bold; and with the headline and first sentence they say everything that needs to be said about the product.

Example
Because he only has a limited amount of space to play with, Peter Jackson, the plumber, decides to use just bullet points in his ads. For his *Yellow Pages* ad, these would read:

- All work guaranteed

- Reasonable rates

- Member of the Institute of Plumbing

- Corgi registered gas installer

- Fast service

- All kinds of work undertaken.

Using flashes

As explained in chapter 5, flashes come in all shapes and sizes, and can be used for a number of purposes. What they all have in common, however, is that in order to be effective, the message inside them must be short. Because of their limited size and shape you can't put too many words in them without having to use a very small typeface; and if you do that, they lose their impact.

Given this limitation, they are usually used in advertising to show prices or savings. Half Price, Just £14.99, and Save £15, for example, are the ideal length for a flash. But they can be used to give *any* message more impact and immediacy, provided it can be conveyed in a few words. Once Only Offer, New Design, Just Out are just a few of the ways in which flashes can be used.

A corner flash, which goes across the corner of the ad, can usually carry a slightly longer message than one in the body of the ad. If you make a starburst or oval flash too big, it can look out of proportion to the other elements, whereas you can get a bit more space across a corner without it becoming too prominent.

Example
The headline in Mary Davies's September ad is concerned with the hobby market, but she wants people to know that she stocks all the textbooks for the Adult Education Centre's classes as well. So she adds a corner flash to the September ad, which says:

All Evening Class Textbooks in Stock Now.

Fig. 21. Bullet points can be used instead of body copy.

Although she did not allow for this in her layout, it can very easily be accommodated at artwork stage by moving the name and address of her shop slightly to the left.

Example
Vidco have allowed for an oval flash in their layout, in which they plan to show the price of each video.

CHECKLIST

- Will *your* headline make an impact on your readers in one and a half seconds?

- Is it pithy, without unnecessary adjectives?

- Does it make a comparison with your competitors? If so, are you in danger of becoming involved in a slanging match?

- Have you involved the reader through an invitation or a question headline?

- Do you have a list of points that can be made in the form of bullet points?

- Do you have a short additional message that lends itself to inclusion in a flash?

7
The Skill of Copywriting

Only one in five people who read your headline are likely to get as far as reading your body copy, but that doesn't mean that body copy is unimportant. The twenty per cent of readers who *do* read it are that much more interested in your product – they are *real* prospects. So it is worth spending time making sure that you get your message across to them.

It isn't necessary to be 'good' at English in order to write advertising copy. In fact, if you are too clever, it can be a positive disadvantage. You just need to be articulate, and to be able to express yourself clearly.

SOME GENERAL COPYWRITING TIPS

The first priority is to decide *what* you want to say. Then you can start thinking about *how* to say it.

Note down what you want to say, forgetting about style, grammar or punctuation for the moment. Once you have got the main points down, start polishing it – rearrange the structure, change some of the words, concentrate on the punctuation, cut it, until it is as readable, persuasive and concise as you can make it.

The importance of each word
Your copy should make an impact, and this means making every word count. A useful exercise, particularly when you are just starting copywriting, is to write out your copy and then see how many words you can cut before it loses its impact. You will be surprised how many words you don't actually need.

Structuring lengthy copy
This doesn't mean that you can't have a lot of copy. Far from it. A brochure, for example, will often *need* a lot of copy. But even then every word matters.

With long copy, you need to pay particular attention to the structure, so that it doesn't become boring, and to the layout. It is a good idea to break up long passages with cross-heads or illustrations. We looked at cross-heads in the last chapter, but you can also add eye-appeal with little drawings scattered around the ad to break up the text. When doing this, however, be sure that the drawings don't interfere with the flow of the words. Don't scatter them randomly; put them in where there's a natural break in the copy.

Presentation of copy

If you are working on a DTP system and doing your own design, you will no doubt type in your own copy, and adjust and amend it as necessary, on your machine. But even if you are using a typesetter or having your ad professionally designed, you should still type your copy. Typesetters and designers don't like working with handwritten copy, and with good reason; it is often difficult and time-consuming to decipher other people's handwriting, and a great many errors can arise as a result.

When presenting copy to a typesetter or designer, it should be double-spaced, and there should be ample margins left and right for any corrections or typesetter's marks and instructions. Anything you want set in bold type should be underlined with a wavy line, like this: bold. And anything you want set in italic type should be underlined with a straight line, like this: italic. Although italic and bold type are now available on word processors, it is still better to use the conventional marks to avoid any confusion.

PLANNING THE CONTENT

It should by now be easy to decide what to say. You have all your product's benefits listed in front of you, and they should form the basis of what you write. Here are some tips on what to include and what to avoid.

- Present facts and arguments, not clichés and waffle.

- Include prices where possible.

- If you have a better product than your competitors, say so, with arguments to prove it.

- Don't use too many superlatives. No one believes them any more.

- Quotations from literature, etc seldom work. Don't, for example, start an ad with 'Tomorrow and tomorrow and tomorrow, creeps in this petty pace from day to day', trying to make the point that your reader should act now. *You* might know that is a quote from *Macbeth*. Most of your readers will be totally baffled – and bored stiff. Quotes from experts (a good review of a book or play, for example) are different. These are **endorsements** and should be highlighted.

- Avoid puns – if your readers don't have your sense of humour (and most of them won't) it is quickest way to lose them.

- If you include testimonials from satisfied customers, separate them from the rest of the copy, either physically or by using a different type. But if you are using testimonials, bear in mind the requirements of the British Code of Advertising Practice outlined in chapter 2.

DEVELOPING YOUR STYLE

Choosing your style
Your style will depend to a large extent on what you are selling, and what your appeal is going to be. There are four main categories of copy style:

- **Emotive**. This is copy which appeals directly to the reader's emotions – self-assertion, love, security, acquisitiveness, etc. 'Be the envy of all your friends...'

- **Factual**. This simply tells the audience about the product, with facts, figures and illustrations. 'Thirty per cent extra with every packet.'

- **Narrative**. Copy in this style tells a story – perhaps of how the product is made, or how it is used, or what your life will be like when *you* use it. 'Last year Linda chose Greece. This year...'

- **Conversational**. This involves a conversation or question and answer session between two people in the ad. 'The neighbours are up to their old tricks again...'

Many ads combine two or more of these styles. A factual ad, for example, can include an appeal to the emotions, or a conversational style can be used to bring out a number of facts about the product. The important thing is to decide on your style, or combination of styles, and stick to it throughout the ad.

Tips on style
- Always write in an upbeat way. Remember that you are trying to

persuade people to buy your product, and unless *you* sound enthusiastic in your copy, you have no hope of making your readers enthusiastic.

* Don't oversell your product, or you risk putting people off. You need to strike a balance between being enthusiastic and overselling. The best way to achieve the right balance is to imagine that you are talking to the person you have chosen to epitomise your target market, trying to persuade him or her. What would you say to someone like that?

* Be informal. You want to give the impression of *talking* conversationally to your audience, not writing an essay; use informal words like 'don't' and 'can't' rather than 'do not' or 'cannot'. Don't on the other hand become too colloquial and use slang.

* Use 'you' as much as possible. This makes your audience feel personally involved.

* Repetition is a useful tool in copywriting, as long as it isn't overdone. For example, a holiday hotel might include the following in its ads:

Seaview Court is just two minutes from the beach.
Seaview Court offers menus for all ages and all tastes.
Seaview Court has a babysitting service for when you want to be alone.
Seaview Court has a games room, a sauna and an indoor pool.
Seaview Court is the ideal base for a family holiday.
The repetition of the name of the hotel is one way of making it stick in the reader's mind.

* Alliteration and rhyme can be effective if they are not overdone. Alliteration is the repetition of the same consonant, as with the 'r' in the tongue-twister 'Round the rugged rocks the ragged rascal ran.' You need to be very careful, however, both with alliteration and with rhyme, that you don't use them too often, and that they aren't forced. They must sound natural, as though they happened almost by accident. If you are in any doubt about whether they sound natural or not, *don't* use them. And *don't* write a poem. The sort of rhyme that works is along the lines of 'Don't delay, ring today', not an epic verse extolling the advantages of your product!

- Choose a style to suit the publication you are using. A copy style that works well in *Country Life*, for example, might not work at all in *Practical Woodworking*, and vice versa. Look carefully at the media you have chosen, and see what kind of market they are aiming at, and the style they use.

- Avoid the trap of trying to emphasise what you see as key words or phrases by putting them in capital letters. This merely distracts readers, and they end up reading nothing but a number of disjointed words, not the whole body of text. You can emphasise the ODD WORD like this, or with *italics*, and whole sections of copy can be emphasised in **bold type**. But use this kind of emphasis sparingly. The more you use typographical methods of emphasis, the less impact they have.

STRUCTURING YOUR COPY

The structure of your copy is important. If it is not properly structured, the reader will find it difficult to follow, and will give up.

An example of bad structure

If a computer bureau advertised its services as follows, how many readers would still be trying to make sense of it by the end?

Need Help with Your Accounts?

If you need help with your accounts, why don't you benefit from our experience and expertise, built up over many years, in which we have been able to help a wide range of businesses with their invoicing, payrolls and accounts, including builders, shopkeepers, hotel owners and many more.

We can keep your paperwork in order. This will keep your accountant happy. Our price includes all accounting services – nominal ledger, bank reconciliation, trial balance, full audit trail for your accountant – all of which will reduce your bookkeeping, giving you more time to run your business, and all this for just £30 per month, on top of which extra services can be quoted on request.

All the information is there, but the structure is all wrong: it doesn't flow, because there is no logic in the information. The first and last sentences are too long and convoluted and the middle ones are unnecessarily short and totally lacking in impact. Moreover, the first sentence wastes space as it simply repeats the headline.

An example of good structure

The computer bureau's ad doesn't have to be completely rewritten. It just needs to be pulled into shape.

Need Help with Your Accounts?

Whatever your business, let us provide the experience and expertise you need. Over the years, we have helped hundreds of firms, from builders to hoteliers, with their invoicing, payrolls and accounts.

Letting us take over the hard slog of bookkeeping enables you to concentrate on running your business. Not only that, we will keep your paperwork in order, which will please your accountant and should reduce his fees!

And what will all this cost you? Just £30 per month, which includes all accounting services, including nominal ledger, bank reconciliation, trial balance and full audit trail for your accountant. Naturally, if you want any additional services, we would be happy to provide them. Just let us know, and we will give you a quote.

Apart from a few stylistic changes to make it a little more positive, the main changes are structural. So what are the features of good structure?

The opening sentence

The opening sentence should be short and attention-grabbing. It is part of that all-important first impression, the attention and interest element of the AIDA principle. For this same reason, your opening sentence should not simply repeat what your headline says, but nor should it go off on a totally different tack. In order to maintain the unity which is an essential part of your ad, it should take up where the headline and/or main illustration ends.

Progressing logically

There should be a logical flow through the copy. Let the first sentence follow from the point made in the headline, as in the example above. Then let each new point or idea flow from the one before. In order to achieve this, it might be necessary to group your product's benefits, rather than taking them strictly in order of priority, but it is more important that the copy should flow than that the benefits should be mentioned in the 'right' order.

If you find that some of the points you want to make don't follow easily, you can use certain valuable 'link' words and phrases to connect them, such as:

Fig. 22. Body copy with a logical flow.

- and of course...

- because...

- naturally...

- not only...

- after all...

- and in addition...

- but...

Take a look at the ad in Fig. 22. In this ad, the copy flows easily and logically from one point to the next: from the impact-making first sentence to the fact that the gear is not just for foul weather, to the waistcoats, to the safety harnesses and lifejackets, to the company's Design Council award to its RNLI contract. Each paragraph, each benefit, leads on to the next. And notice the link words and phrases: 'But it's more than...'; 'Take the Multifit Ocean Buoyancy Waistcoat'; 'But Musto Offshore is not only...'; 'Not that you have to be...'.

Constructing sentences

The structure of your copy and the way it flows are also affected by the construction and length of your sentence. How do you construct your sentences? At its most basic, do they have a beginning, a middle and an end? Or do you end your sentences in the middle, leaving the reader unsure of the point you are trying to make? At the other end of the scale, do your sentences go on and on, piling one clause on top of another, one idea on top of another, until the reader is quite dizzy trying to keep track (like the sentences in the first example of the ad for the computer services bureau on page 118).

The basic rule is that each sentence should carry a single idea – and as far as possible, each idea should have a sentence to itself. To say 'Speedy Car Hire is cheapest for weddings. And for fleet hire' disturbs the flow of the idea, which is that Speedy Car Hire are the cheapest. The only time when such a construction would be legitimate would be if you wanted to place special emphasis on the 'And for fleet hire'. Then it would be almost as though there were two ideas.

Sentence length

As we saw in the computer bureau example above, sentences which carry too many different ideas, even though they may be grammatically correct, are cumbersome and hard to follow.

Along with the construction of your sentences you need to consider their length. In advertising the general rule is to keep sentences short. You want to make an impact, which is difficult to achieve with long sentences. Having said that, a long succession of very short sentences, even if they do all carry a different idea, is boring, so you do need to vary the length. Look again at Fig. 22. None of the sentences is very long, but there is variety, which creates interest.

If you find that you can't avoid a succession of short sentences (perhaps there are a number of benefits you want to bring out, and each is in the form of a short sentence), try using bullet points, or change the construction.

Suppose you have woollen cardigans to sell. Your first draft copy might read. 'It comes in a wide range of colours. It is soft. It is stylish.' You could change it to: 'It is soft, stylish, and comes in a wide range of colours.' This is several ideas in one sentence, but it reads better than the original (another example of how the rules of advertising were made to be broken!). Alternatively, you could use **bullet points**:

- more colours
- more style
- more softness.

A third possibility is to turn the copy into an **invitation**:
See the ranges of colours.
Feel the softness.
Enjoy the admiration of your friends.

Which of these options you choose will depend on the style and tone you want to achieve.

Paragraphing

Paragraphing is also important to your structure. Any long body of unbroken text becomes difficult to read. This may not matter much in a complex academic textbook, but in an ad it will just kill interest. So do break up your copy into manageable paragraphs.

Just as each sentence should contain a single idea, so each paragraph should have a single theme or group of ideas — and each theme should be contained in a single paragraph. Once again, however, there will be occasions when you will break this rule. You need to maintain the reader's interest, so your paragraphs should be short. If you find that a particular paragraph is becoming too long, then you may need to break it up, even though each new paragraph may not cover a complete theme. You might also decide to form a paragraph from a single sentence, in order to give it emphasis.

As with sentences, however, variety is the key. A succession of short, single-sentence paragraphs can be as counter-productive as one long boring one. If you *do* have a lot of short, unrelated points to make, use bullet points. Copy needs to flow, and a lot of very short paragraphs interferes with that flow.

The closing sentence – be positive

Your closing sentence is almost as important a part of the structure of your copy as the opening one, and it pays to consider it before you get too far into your writing. You need to leave your reader with a positive image. The worst thing you can do, having got people interested in your product, is to break off abruptly, as though you have suddenly run out of things to say. Consider how you are going to end your copy *before* you run out of things to say. This is particularly important if you don't have a slogan to sign off with, but even if you do, your closing sentence still needs careful thought.

Your closing sentence should do one of five things.

• Tell people how they can get the product

• Point out one more benefit

• Summarise the rest of the copy

• Make a link with the headline

• Act as a slogan.

If yours is a direct response ad, then the closing sentence almost writes itself. It will invite people to send off for the product. Even if it isn't a direct response ad, you can still tell people how to get your product – 'Available in all good bookshops', 'Look out for it next time you're shopping', 'Give us a ring for a free quote today' all invite action.

Keeping one of your list of benefits until last, you can end on a high note. Plan your copy carefully if you want to do this, because you will need a benefit which is going to leave the reader feeling really good about your product while flowing naturally from the rest of the copy.

Your closing sentence can also just 'round off' your copy by summarising your points and arguments in one succinct sentence.

Example

A garage might explain in its copy that it offers a variety of services, and that it is fast, efficient and friendly. It could then close with: 'So whatever your needs, for fast, reliable, personal service, come to Brown's Motor Services.'

If your headline makes a claim which your body copy sets out to prove then your closing sentence can link with it to show that you have proved your points. The ad in Fig. 22, for example, has the headline 'You can't beat the system.' The copy then explains why Musto Offshore is unbeatable. The last sentence then picks up the wording of the headline to say 'Musto Offshore. You can't beat it.' This form of closing sentence *implies* that you have proved your point. But you could be more explicit.

Example

An electrical shop might advertise with a headline

The Best Deal in Town.

The copy would then explain *why* it is the best deal – better quality goods, lower prices, money-back guarantee. The closing sentence could be: 'Now, isn't that the best deal in town?'

If you don't have a slogan as part of your logo, your closing sentence could act as one. However, if you do have a slogan, don't invent another one as a closing sentence, as it will probably be wasted. Find another way of ending your copy.

Designing coupons

If yours is a direct response ad, then you will usually need a coupon or order form for readers to complete and return. There are some key points to remember when designing one. You want to get as many people as possible to send in coupons. You therefore need to make it as easy as possible for them to do so. How?

- Always ensure that the coupon is at the edge of the page of the magazine or newspaper so that it is easy to cut out. If your ad is a top left-hand quarter-page, don't put your coupon in the bottom right-hand corner of the ad. It makes it difficult to cut without cutting up the whole page. (You will have to specify the position in which you want your ad to appear when reserving your space.)

- Give the customer enough space to fill in all the details you need clearly and legibly. Don't just allow an inch or two for the address, for example. Either people won't bother to complete it, or they will write so small that you won't be able to read it.

- Make it absolutely clear what information you need from them, and how to complete the coupon. If they are ordering actual goods, ensure that the ordering instructions are clear and that there is sufficient space for them to insert the information you need to process the order. If there is any possibility of your readers being confused, you can guarantee many of them will be!

The golden rule is, the easier you make it for readers to return your coupons, the more people will.

CHOOSING THE RIGHT WORDS

The words you choose for your copy are very important. There are some words which trigger the right reactions, others which will simply put the reader off. In fact words which in some contexts and media provoke one kind of reaction, will have quite the opposite effect in others.

Reference books

Many copywriters advocate that you shouldn't have any reference books with you when writing your copy, as it merely encourages you to use words that you would not normally use. I disagree. There are two types of book that are indispensable to anyone who is going to be writing more than the most basic copy. One is a simple dictionary, and the other is a dictionary of synonyms.

A dictionary is essential not only to check spellings, but also to ensure that some of the words you use actually mean what you think they mean. It is surprising how many everyday words people use in the wrong context, and you will simply irritate many readers if you do that.

A synonym dictionary can be very useful in two ways. First, it is off-putting for the reader if you use the same word over and over again. If you are selling designs for do-it-yourself furniture, for example, you shouldn't keep saying 'The designs are... The designs do... There are so many designs to choose from.' But what other word do you use? A synonym dictionary will tell you. It will also help you if you are stuck for the right word. How many times have you had a word on the tip of your tongue – just the word you need to express what you want to say – but not been able to think of it? You can think of any number of words which have a similar meaning, but not the precise one. A synonym dictionary will help you find it.

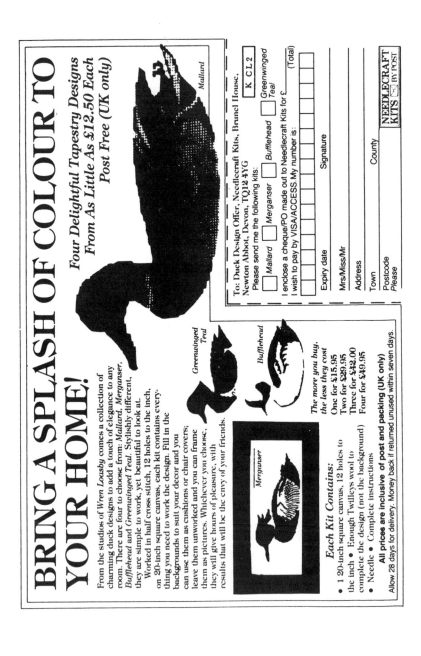

BRING A SPLASH OF COLOUR TO YOUR HOME!

Four Delightful Tapestry Designs From As Little As £12.50 Each Post Free (UK only)

From the studios of *Wren Loasby* comes a collection of charming duck designs to add a touch of elegance to any room. There are four to choose from: *Mallard*, *Merganser*, *Bufflehead* and *Greenwinged Teal*. Stylishly different, they are simple to work, yet beautiful to look at.

Worked in half cross stitch, 12 holes to the inch, on 20-inch square canvas, each kit contains everything you need to work the design. Fill in the backgrounds to suit your decor and you can use them as cushions or chair covers; leave them unworked and you can frame them as pictures. Whichever you choose, they will give hours of pleasure, with results that will be the envy of your friends.

Each Kit Contains:
- 1 20-inch square canvas, 12 holes to the inch • Enough Twilleys wool to complete the design (not the background)
- Needle • Complete instructions

All prices are inclusive of post and packing (UK only)
Allow 28 days for delivery. Money back if returned unused within seven days.

The more you buy, the less they cost
One for £15.95
Two for £29.95
Three for £42.00
Four for £49.95

Mallard

Greenwinged Teal

Bufflehead

Merganser

Fig. 23. Key words used appropriately to the image of the journal in this case *Country Living*.

126

Using the right words to get the right reaction

There are certain key words which will always attract interest. Possibly the most obvious is 'free'! Here are a few more:

- now
- introducing
- announcing
- secret
- magic
- unique
- latest
- sale
- bargain.

The list can be expanded, but those are probably the most important. Use them when appropriate to get people to read your copy, but like all advertising devices, don't overdo them, or they will have the opposite effect.

Remember, words that might get just the right reaction in certain circumstances and certain media won't necessarily work in others; in the same way that you tailor your *style* to the media you are using, so you must choose the right *words*.

The ad in Fig. 23 shows this. It appeared in *Country Living*, an up-market magazine with a fairly sophisticated readership. Notice the use of words like 'elegance', 'stylishly different' and 'decor' – words that suit the image of the magazine. Had the ad been written for a different publication, the style and the descriptive words would have been different, for example 'attractive', 'popular', and 'cheap'.

GRAMMAR AND PUNCTUATION

There are times when, to achieve a particular effect, you need to bend, or even break, the normal rules of grammar and punctuation. That is perfectly acceptable; you can stick *too* rigidly to the rules. But there is a difference between breaking the rules of grammar for a particular reason and just ignoring them. There is no value in being ungrammatical through sheer laziness. Your ad will simply look slipshod and amateurish.

Some basic rules of grammar

This is not the place for a grammar lesson, and if you are worried about the quality of your written English, there are a number of guides to good grammar available. But there are three very basic rules well worth following:

- A sentence needs a **subject** and a **predicate**. The subject is the person or thing the sentence is about, and the predicate tells us something about the subject. The predicate must contain a verb – a 'doing' word. So in the sentence 'We offer the best value in town', the subject is 'we' (that's who the sentence is about) and the predicate is 'offer the best value in town', which includes the verb 'offer'.

- If a sentence has several sections, each with its own verb, these sections are called **clauses**; they may be separated by punctuation marks – commas, semicolons or dashes, but *not* full stops. They may also be introduced by conjunctions – 'and, 'but', 'who', 'which' etc. A common mistake is to write something like: 'Come to us for quality service. Which cannot be bettered.' The second part of this passage is a subsidiary clause describing the service, and is therefore part of the first sentence. So it should read: 'Come to us for quality service which cannot be bettered.'

- Make sure that words, phrases or clauses which describe people or things are placed as close to them as possible, otherwise you will cause confusion as to what they refer to. For example, 'Visiting Spain, our staff will be pleased to advise you' gives the impression that the company's staff are visiting Spain! The right way to express that is to say 'If you are visiting Spain, our staff will be pleased to advise you.'

There are occasions when you might want to break even these basic rules. An English teacher, for example, would mark the following wrong: 'We have never been undersold. Ever.' 'Ever' is not a sentence. But in advertising terms, it is not only often acceptable, it is a useful device for giving emphasis to the point. And many of the rules of punctuation can and should be broken. When writing an essay, you would break up sentences with semicolons. In advertising, you are more likely to do so with dashes, as they have more immediacy, more impact. Advertising is not only a literary exercise, it is also a visual one.

When you think your copy is as good as you can make it, leave it overnight, and look at it again critically in the morning. Does it still sound good? If so, it probably is.

CASE STUDIES

Mary drafts copy and bullets points
Mary hasn't allowed for much copy, as she doesn't feel she needs very

much. She decides she needs about fifty-five words of actual body copy and thirty-five words for the bullet points.

Her first draft for the September ad reads as follows:

> In our spacious, well-lit shop, we stock the widest range of practical leisure books in the area. We also have a good range of school supplies, reference books and revision aids, and stock all the recommended books of the Adult Education Centre's evening classes. So come and browse – you'll be surprised what you might find.

There is nothing wrong with the basic structure of this copy – the sentences make sense, they are not too long, and it follows through. It isn't very exciting, though, and it has one important flaw: the first sentence doesn't follow on from the headline. It goes off at a tangent, talking about the shop. So Mary does two things. She rewrites some of it to make it a bit more punchy and changes the order slightly.

This is how it looks after her changes:

> From sewing to stamp collecting, modelling to music, we have the widest range of leisure books in the area. Whatever your hobby, if there's a book on it, the chances are we've got it.
>
> Our spacious, well-lit shop is ideal for browsing, so do call in – you'll be surprised at what you find.

She then puts the rest of her benefits in bullet point form.

- We have a wide range of school supplies.

- We also stock novels, biographies, travel books and a whole lot more.

- We will order any book you want at no extra charge.

Peter writes a sales letter

The copy for Peter Jackson's ads is easy to do, as it simply consists of bullet points listing the benefits he offers, as shown in chapter 5. His sales letter, on the other hand, takes a bit of thought. Sales letters can have a heading, but they often don't, and Peter decides to do without one. Apart from that difference, writing his sales letter is very similar to writing copy for an ad. He writes as follows:

Dear Mr

Do you need a fully qualified plumber for subcontract work? I can offer a full service at very reasonable rates.

I am a good timekeeper, punctual and reliable, and I pride myself on the quality of my work. As a Member of the Institute of Plumbing and a Corgi registered gas installer, I am able to handle any job, from the simplest to the most complicated.

Although I am now self-employed, I was until recently employed by Mr James Green of J. Green & Sons, 43 Beech Road, Woodham, and he will, I am sure, confirm that my work is of the highest standard.

I look forward to hearing from you if you think you could use my services.

Yours sincerely,

Peter Jackson

The video makers

Vidco need to write about sixty words of general copy, selling the videos as a concept, and then about twenty-five words on each video. Their copy looks like this:

Improving your golf the Vidco way is like having a professional right in your living room – only considerably less expensive! In these high-quality videos, top players give you the benefit of their expert advice, and show you step by step how each shot should be played.
AND WE GUARANTEE that if you're not completely satisfied, we'll refund your money – no quibble, no delay.

The Drive
Addressing the tee ... the stance ... correcting a slice or a hook ... Joe Driver helps you make every drive a winner.

The Approach Shot
Peter Irons, renowned for his ability to get himself out of tricky situations, shows you how to cope on the fairway – and off it!

The Putt
From adopting the right attitude and assessing your approach to sinking the shot, David Putter explains how to play this most difficult of shots.

The coupon reads:

For a Better Way to Learn, Post This Coupon Today

To: Vidco Ltd., 35 Church Road, Barchester, AB1 2CD.

Please send me the following videos:

The Drive	... copies @ £29.99 each ...
The Approach Shot	... copies @ £29.99 each ...
The Putt	... copies @ £29.99 each ...
Please add £3.00 for postage and packing	£3.00
TOTAL	...

* I enclose a cheque/postal order, payable to Vidco Ltd.
* Please charge my Access/Visa account. My card number is
is .... Expiry date: .... Signature: ....
*Delete as necessary.

The riding centre
The Talbots go through the same process as they did with their headlines; they write several drafts of their copy before coming up with what they like. Their final copy for the January/February ads looks like this:

Come to Happy Valley Riding Centre for:

• Riding, trekking, schooling and a great deal more

• A country holiday just five minutes from the sea

• Friendly service and reasonable prices

• Self-catering or full-board accommodation.

Want to know more? Send for our brochure.
Happy Valley Riding Centre, Riverside, Near Downton, Dyfed.
Tel. Downton 123456

[STARTING A NEW HOBBY?] *18 pt Helvetica bold, centred*

[We have a book on it.] *14 pt Helvetica bold, centred.*

From sewing to stamp collecting,
modelling to music, we have the widest
range of leisure books in the area.
And if you're starting an evening
class, we stock the recommended books
for those as well.

Our spacious, well-lit shop is ideal
for browsing, so do call in - you'll be
surprised at what you find.

9/10 pt Century

* We have a wide range of school supplies
* We also stock novels, biographies,
  travel books and a whole lot more
* We will order any book you want at
  no extra charge

9/10 pt Century Bold

[MERCHESTER BOOKSHOP] *10 pt Helvetica bold, centred*

[High Street
Merchester] *9 pt Helvetica bold, centred*

Fig. 24. Copy marked up and ready for the typesetter.

For the autumn ads, they use more or less the same copy, except that they replace 'Friendly service and reasonable rates' with 'Special rates for weekend and winter breaks', and put it at the top of their list.

The copy for the brochure is what takes the most time – partly because there is more of it, but also because it needs careful planning. On the inside they start with some introductory copy emphasising the choice of activities, and tie it in with the headline on the front with the words: 'And the difference? The difference is that we offer superb facilities for the non-rider as well.'

They then go on to devote a paragraph to expanding on each of the cross-heads they had decided on. So under 'In the Heart of the Country Yet Close to the Sea', they describe their situation. Under 'Riding and Trekking', they set out the facilities they offer for both group and individual outings. Under 'Schooling, Jumping and Dressage', they point out that they have an indoor and an outdoor school. Under 'Riding Holidays With a Difference', they discuss the facilities for non-riding activities. And under 'The Centre', they describe the accommodation and social facilities.

On the back they write about the Mid-Wales area in general, its beauty, its charming towns and its spectacular scenery.

SENDING COPY TO THE TYPESETTER

Having typed out your copy, it goes to the typesetter or designer to be set, unless you're working on a DTP system. But of course, they can't tell just from a typewritten sheet how you want it laid out. You can either talk to them about it and explain what you want, or you can mark it up yourself. It is not difficult to do, as Fig. 24 shows, and it avoids any confusion.

Marking up copy

Words to be set in italics or in bold should already be marked as explained at the beginning of the chapter. If you are using a designer then that is all that's necessary. If, however, you are briefing a typesetter yourself, you need to tell him the typeface and the size of type you want for each section of the ad. Simply bracket the particular piece you are referring to, and write against it 'Century (the typeface), 9/10 point (the type size, and leading).'

You can also indicate the **measure** (the length of each line), but it is probably easier to supply the typesetter with a copy of your layout, and let him work out the measure for himself – especially if there are a number of different measures in the ad. Any lines to be centred (your heading for example) should be enclosed in square brackets [ ], as shown in Fig. 24. For more on dealing with typesetters, see chapter 9.

CHECKLIST

- Is the style of your copy right for your market, and for the media in which you are advertising?

- Is it enthusiastic enough? But have you gone over the top?

- Have you set out all the benefits being sold?

- Are there words you can cut without losing impact?

- Does the opening sentence grab the attention?

- Does the rest of the copy flow logically from one point to the next?

- Do your sentences each contain a single clear idea? Have your varied their length?

- Does each paragraph follow a logical theme?

- Does the closing sentence round the copy off, or does it leave the reader 'hanging'?

- Have you chosen the right sort of words for your market?

- Is the copy grammatical? If not is there a good reason?

8
Putting it All Together

Now you have to put everything together into your **artwork**. Properly called **camera-ready artwork**, this consists of all the elements of the ad, all in their proper places, ready to be photographed for the printing process. If you are working on a DTP system, then the artwork will take shape as you work, rather than being a separate stage in the process. All you have to do is print it out. But if you are working by hand, then all the elements of the ad will come together at this stage.

What is required here is an eye for detail, an eye for colour if you are using it, a steady hand and a degree of creativity. You will also need a few pieces of basic equipment.

If you did your own layout, you can probably put together your own artwork; otherwise you will have to find a professional designer, as suggested in chapter 9. If you used a designer at layout stage, the designer will normally do the artwork as well. Many newspapers and local directories employ staff who will do the artwork for you but, as with any designer, check their cost and quality before you commit yourself.

BASIC ARTWORK EQUIPMENT

You could get by with just a few basic items of equipment:

- A drawing board. This needn't be a sophisticated piece of furniture costing a fortune. A piece of solid level board of at least 700 x 500mm is really all you need. You could use a desk, but it is likely to get a bit messy, so a special board would be better.

- White art paper or board on which to stick all the pieces of artwork. If you are preparing a brochure, you will need a separate piece for each double-page spread.

- Some tape to secure the art paper or board to the drawing board, so that it doesn't slip around while you are working on it. It can be extremely frustrating, if you are nine-tenths of your way through a job, to have the paper slip, and your lines go crooked!

- A T-square, a ruler and a set square to help you draw accurate vertical and horizontal lines. If you are also likely to want to draw lines at odd angles, a protractor would be useful. Apart from the T-square, which you should be able to get for a few pounds from an art shop, the other items are part of any basic geometry set.

- A pair of compasses and dividers. The compasses are indispensable for drawing circles, and dividers will help you divide lines into equal parts. These can also be found in a geometry set.

- A light blue pencil for drawing the dimensions of the ad or any guidelines – lines which are for guidance only, and are not to appear in the ad (when the artwork is photographed, light blue pencil lines won't show up). You can also use your blue pencil to draw in any rules or design elements to be inked in later with a drawing or felt-tipped pen when you are sure they are right.

- A black technical drawing pen and black felt- or fibre-tipped pens of different thicknesses for drawing in any lines and rules to be printed.

- Correcting fluid will come in useful for any small mistakes you may make when inking them in.

- Scissors and/or a scalpel. It's best to use a scalpel for cutting out the various elements that make up your artwork. Scissors will do, but they are not as easy to use as a scalpel, nor do they give as clean a cut.

- Tweezers are good for handling small, fiddly pieces of artwork.

- Adhesive for sticking everything down. There are various kinds available, from the ubiquitous Cow Gum to spray-on glue. You can choose whichever one suits you best, but remember that if you get some adhesives on areas which are not to be glued, they can look dirty and show up when photographed. Rubber cement is useful here. If you go over the area to be glued, the excess can be removed with a ball of dried Cow Gum.

- Tracing or overlay paper is useful for covering and protecting your artwork and illustrations, as well as for your overlay, if you use one.

- If you are using colour, a tint chart will help you specify the colours you want for various elements in your ad. They are very expensive to buy, however, so you might prefer to use your printer's chart.

ARTWORK TECHNIQUES

Preparing your working surface
First tape your working surface to your drawing board so that it doesn't move while you are working. Then use your T-square and set square to mark out the printing area – the outside line of your ad. If you have a border, a line around the ad, then draw the line in black. If not, draw the edge of the area to be printed in light blue pencil, so that it doesn't show up when photographed. Your working surface should be big enough to have a 50mm margin all around the printing area.

If you are doing a brochure, use this margin to draw the various reference marks for the printer *in black*. These are the **trim lines** and any **fold lines**.

- Trim lines are lines at the four corners of the printing area, which show the printer where to trim or cut the brochure to size.

- Similarly, the fold lines indicate where it is to be folded.

Fig. 25 shows examples of these lines. Note that trim lines are solid, while fold lines are dotted; both are kept *outside* the printing area.

Now draw, with your blue pencil again, where each element is to go. Refer to your layout, making sure that you get each piece in exactly the right position. Use your T-square, ruler and set square (and protractor if necessary) to ensure that your lines are straight and your angles correct. Don't worry if you overdraw, or if you make a mistake. The lines won't photograph.

It is best to start with your key element first – it may be your main illustration or your headline or a particularly complicated picture; once you have got that right, relate the rest to it.

Laying down the artwork
Now you are ready to put it all together. Do it one step at a time, and you should have no problems.

1. Draw in any **rules** or **keylines**, in black. Rules are straight lines to be printed, such as a 'box' around a particular piece of text, or a line dividing one part of the ad from another. Keylines are usually also straight lines, but they are there just to indicate divisions between

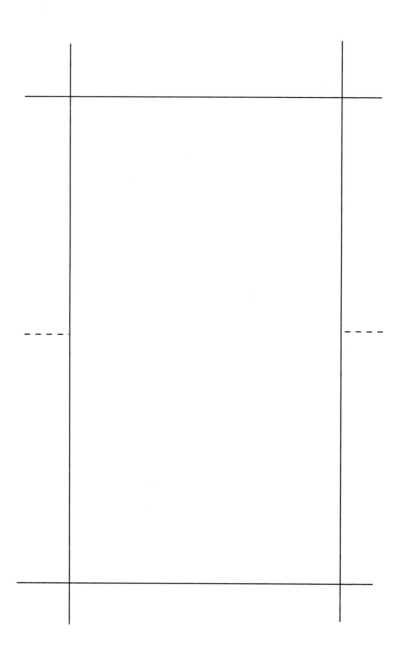

Fig. 25. Printing area (to be drawn in blue), showing trim lines (solid) and fold lines (dotted). These lines should be drawn in black.

one colour and another. For example, if you want a particular panel to be printed in cerise while the rest of the background is pink, you would draw a keyline around it, and indicate on your **overlay** (see later under 'Colour') which colours are to go where.

2. If the line drawings are the right size, paste them down one at a time; make sure that they are in exactly the right position and at the right angle, using your T-square to ensure that they are correctly aligned. Cover them with a piece of tracing paper and press down firmly. If they have to be **enlarged** to **reduced** to fit, then just mark where they are to go on the artwork at the enlarged or reduced size, and supply the original drawings to the printer separately.

3. Unless the photographer has supplied **reference prints** (see later under 'Illustrations'), do *not* paste down any photographs. Simply draw a solid line around each photograph's precise position, and supply the photographs to the printer separately. Number each position, and write the corresponding number on the back of each photograph. Paste down any reference prints into their correct position.

4. Lay down the typeset text, *unpasted*. The typesetter should have set the text to the right measure for each section, but if your layout is complicated you may have to cut it with your scalpel to fit it round the illustrations or logo. If, despite your calculations, the typeset copy is too long to fit (and it does happen), you should be able to cut out a line or two before pasting. Make sure that you cut it absolutely parallel with the lines of text so that it will fit easily onto your guidelines. When you are satisfied that it is right for the space allowed, paste it down.

5. If you plan to use flashes, you can buy sheets of different kinds from an art shop, and simply transfer them to the artwork, pasting them down in the correct position.

HANDLING ILLUSTRATIONS

Reference prints

The photographer might give you reference prints of any shots he has taken. These are black and white prints which are exactly the right size and shape for the ad. They can't be reproduced by the printer, but it is useful to have them – you can then paste them down so that the printer knows exactly where each photograph is to go, its angle etc, and there is no chance of any confusion. If your layout is at all complicated, insist on

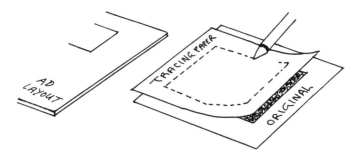

1. Trace outline of original on overlay paper.

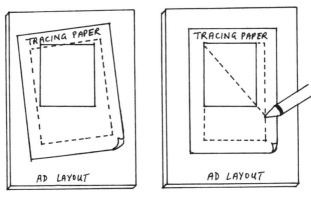

2. Position top left corner of overlay with top left corner of ad layout picture area.

3. Trace diagonal line over ad layout picture area until it bisects outline on overlay.

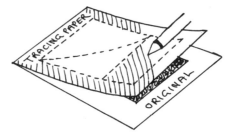

4. Crop off unwanted area of original picture by shading overlay.

Fig. 26. Cropping an illustration.

getting reference prints from your photographer (see chapter 9).

If you are working with existing photographs, however, there won't be any reference prints, so you will have nothing to paste down; it then becomes even more vital to indicate the positioning precisely. Some DTP systems allow you to scan in illustrations. These serve the same purpose in DTP-produced artwork as reference prints do in the manual variety. But you still need to provide the printer with the originals.

Processing photographs

Provide the printer with the original photographs, not negatives. Colour photographs can be supplied either as transparencies or colour prints, and black and white photographs as prints.

The printer can't print straight from your photographs. Whether they are in colour or black and white, he will need to process them first. Colour pictures have to be **scanned**, and separated into the different primary colours (see 'Colour' below), each of which is then printed separately. Even your black and white photographs have to be processed. Your printer will use them to make **half-tones**, converting the full-tone image into a mass of tiny black and white dots of varying intensity to achieve the shades of black, white and grey.

The printer should return all prints, transparencies and artwork to you with the finished job.

Cropping

You may have photographs (or even line drawings) which are the wrong shape or size, or which contain elements you don't want or need in your ad. If a picture is the wrong shape, or if you want to remove part of it, you will need to **crop** it. This means instructing the printer to 'cut' a certain section when reproducing it. Here's how to crop a photograph:

1. Trace the outline of the picture onto a piece of tracing paper.

2. Put the trace over your layout, so that one corner of the outline matches one corner of the space you have allowed for the picture on the layout.

3. Draw a diagonal line from that corner to the opposite corner of the space on the layout and extend it until it meets the edge of the picture's outline. This will be the extent of the final image. The rest will have to be cropped.

4. Shade the section to be excluded on the tracing paper, and place it over the picture, keeping it in place with tape along the top edge, so that the printer knows exactly where to crop.

Fig. 27. Making a cut-out of the model in the ad on page 62.

Sizing

You will often find yourself working with illustrations which are the wrong size – either too small or too big. You will therefore have to **size** them. Sometimes, as with the example in Fig. 26, a picture will need cropping *and* sizing. Sizing involves telling the printer how much bigger or smaller you want the final image to be, expressed as a percentage.

The calculation is quite simple. First get the original photograph to the right shape, if necessary, by cropping. Then measure one dimension (height or width, it doesn't matter) of the space you have allowed for the final image, and the corresponding dimension of the original illustration. The calculation is then as follows:

$$\text{size of final image} \div \text{size of original} \times 100$$

Suppose the space of your layout is 75mm high, and the height of the original photograph is 150mm; the calculation is $75 \div 150 \times 100$, which is 50. You then simply write on the back of the original photograph, or on a piece of overlay, '50%'. Suppose it was the other way round, and the space on the layout was 150mm high while the photograph was only 75mm high; it would then be $150 \div 75 \times 100$, which is 200. So you would write on your photograph, '200%'.

One word of warning: any enlargement over 1000% will look blurred, so make sure that the right format is used for the photograph. If you need a big picture, use 5inch x 4inch not 35mm.

Cut-out and overlaid photographs

The printer also needs clear instructions about any **cut-out** photographs you want. These are illustrations without any background, such as the model shown in Fig. 7. You should still send the whole photograph. Put an overlay on it, and trace round the outline of the item or items you want to show. As with cropping, shade anything that is to be left out (see Fig. 27).

Also make clear to the printer how you want **overlaid** illustrations shown. These are pictures which cut into each other, so as to give an effect of overlapping. Indicate clearly on your artwork which image is to be 'on top', and by how much it is to overlap.

PRINTING IN COLOUR

In colour printing, each colour has to be printed separately. For this reason advertising uses just four basic colours, known as the **process colours**:

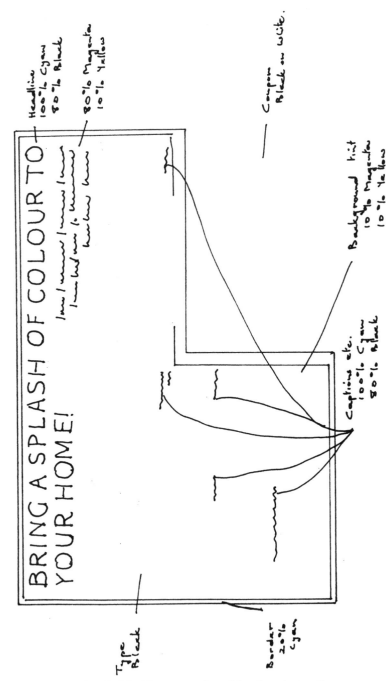

Fig. 28. Marking an overlay with colour instructions
for the artwork in Fig. 23.

- yellow
- magenta (a red colour)
- cyan (a bright blue)
- black (sometimes referred to as k).

These four colours can be combined by the printer in an almost endless variety of ways to form almost any other colour imaginable.

Using colour in your ad doesn't just mean using colour photographs. Indeed, if you leave all the rest of your ad black and white it is almost a waste of money. You are paying for full-colour printing, but not making full use of it. You could have a dark blue headline, burgundy cross-heads, the coupon in pale green and a yellow tint behind the bullet points. (The ad would look pretty horrific, but you *could* have them!)

A sense of colour is useful if you are doing your own artwork for a colour ad. The main thing is to ensure that the colours and combinations you choose are in keeping with the image you are trying to create. More muted colours are obviously better for a quieter, more staid image.

Specifying tints

Colour photographs are **scanned** by the printer to separate out the four process colours. For the rest of the ad you need to specify what shades you want. For this you will need a tint chart. You can buy one, but they are expensive and if you are doing a brochure your printer probably has one that you can use.

Tints are specified in terms of the basic process colours they contain, expressed as percentages. As with black and white half-tones, colour inks are applied through a screen, and the percentage you specify determines how dense the resulting dots are, and therefore how dark the colour is. So '100% yellow, 100% cyan', for example, means that both solid yellow and solid cyan are used, which gives you a bright leaf green. On the other hand, '20% yellow, 20% magenta' means that the colour 'dots' are well spaced out, with a lot of white in between, giving you a much paler colour – in this case peach. You can combine three colours if you like; 10% yellow, 20% cyan, 20% magenta, for example, produces lilac.

Your tint chart shows you what every combination of the basic colours will look like, so that you can choose which shades you want to use, and see what you need to specify in order to get them. The percentages usually increase in multiples of 10%.

Having decided on the colours for each element of your ad, how do you specify them? Just put an overlay of tracing paper over the artwork (fold it over the top and tape it onto the back, to keep it in place), trace out the elements or the keylines of the areas you want colour in, and mark on the overlay what tints and colours are to be used for each. Fig. 28 shows an overlay specifying colours for the ad in Fig. 23.

THE NEXT STEP

Protecting artwork
Protect your valuable artwork and any photographs or illustrations which are being sent loose. The best thing is to paste each item onto a piece of board to keep it rigid, and tape a protective paper overlay to the front.

Identify everything
Make sure that everything is identified, that the illustrations which you are sending loose are correctly numbered, and that any cropping, reduction or enlargement is clearly indicated.

If you are sending the ad to a publication, write a covering letter indicating the issue it is to go into, its position and size, your space order number and the reference of any confirmation of order you received.

Use a large envelope, preferably padded and strengthened to avoid damage in the post, and send it by registered post or Datapost – it would be tragic if everything was mislaid at this stage!

Do the same if you are sending brochure artwork to a printer. If your printer is local, of course, you can take everything to him and explain your needs in person.

CHECKLIST

- Have you got the good eye and steady hand necessary to do your own artwork if you are not using a DTP system?

- Have you got the basic equipment for the job?

- Are all lines for guidance only drawn in light blue pencil?

- Are the trim and fold lines of your brochure on the outside of the print area?

- Have you drawn the lines where each element is to go in light blue pencil, to be inked in when you are sure they are right?

- Are you sure all the elements fit in before you paste them down?

- Do you know how to crop any illustrations which are the wrong shape, and size any which are the wrong size?

- If you are using colour, what colours will suit your ad best, and do you know how to specify them?

9
Dealing with the Professionals

You should find the professionals you have to deal with, from designers to printers, helpful and accommodating. After all, they are trying to sell you their services. However, it is as well to know what to expect from them, what they should be doing for you and what your own responsibilities are, to avoid misunderstanding.

FINDING THE RIGHT PROFESSIONAL

The first place to look for professional help is in the relevant section of *Yellow Pages*.

- Designers   'Designers – advertisers and graphic'.

- Picture libraries   'Photograph libraries'.

- Photographers   'Photographers – commercial and industrial'.

- Copywriters   Don't have their own classification; you will find them under 'Advertising agencies'.

- Typesetters   'Typesetters'.

- Printers   'Printers and lithographers'.

Yellow Pages is fine for local services, and you will not usually need to go far afield to find the people you need. Some professionals, however, especially picture libraries, photographers and illustrators, concentrate on certain subjects, and if your needs are very specialised you may have to look beyond your immediate vicinity. In that case, the *Creative Handbook* will come in useful. It is expensive, but it is a valuable reference book, as it lists a wide range of advertising specialists throughout the country. If you are unsure about a picture library, the trade association, the British Association of Picture Libraries and Agencies, will be able to provide names and addresses of their members near you.

British Association of Picture Libraries and Agencies
13 Woodberry Crescent
London N10 1PJ.

Finding a specialist through either *Yellow Pages* or the *Creative Handbook* is only the first step, however. Will you be happy with their work? Always ask to see examples of their work, and satisfy yourself that their style and quality really are what you are looking for. Most of the work, especially that of designers, copywriters, illustrators and photographers, is creative in nature, so your reaction to their style will be subjective – either you like it or you don't. If you like it, it will probably be right for you. But as far as technical quality is concerned, here are a few things to watch out for:

- Designers. Visually balanced ads, with no single element over-powering the rest. Not too crowded. A unified message, rather than a collection of disjointed bits and pieces.

- Photographers. Good composition, clarity, and a knowledge of the subject they are photographing.

- Illustrators. A clear, uncluttered style that reproduces without blurring, and a knowledge of the subject they are drawing or painting.

- Copywriters. Imaginative and exciting headlines, and a good flow to the copy.

- Typesetters. Accurate setting, with the absolute minimum of mistakes. A good range of typefaces.

- Printers. Clear printing, with no smudging, spots, or blurring of the letters or pictures. With four-colour work, check especially the quality of the colour reproduction, as many local printers do not really have the facilities for quality colour work. The best results are achieved on big four-colour presses, rather than multiple printing on small one- or two-colour presses.

Jackson Building Supplies

Potters Lane, Seaport

14th August 199X

Catherine Billington
5 Oak Drive
Seaport

PURCHASE ORDER

Please supply:	Black and white artwork for ad to be featured in the SEAPORT CHRONICLE.
Size:	124 x 190mm
Date required:	Basic layout required by 20th August 199X. Completed artwork required by 10th September 199X.
Price:	£40.00 as quoted by you, 12th August 199X.

With compliments

(*Signature*)

Bill Smith
Director

Fig. 29. A sample purchase order.

DEFINING THE JOB

Having found the right specialists, it is important that they should know exactly what you require of them. Many of these people work on a very informal basis – even printers will often undertake a job purely on the basis of a verbal request. It is therefore in your own interests to ensure that everyone knows in detail what you want them to do, and to document things as necessary.

What you want will sometimes only emerge after a long discussion, particularly if you are briefing a designer or copywriter. Many business people are quite happy with a verbal agreement – they discuss the ad with the particular specialist, and then agree on how to proceed. You may prefer to have a written record as a point of reference in case there is any dispute. In that case, you should provide a formal **purchase order**.

With some professionals, such as typesetters and printers, your requirements will be fairly straightforward; they can be specified either on the purchase order or on the material you provide – marked-up copy, for example, or artwork and photographs. But with others, including designers and copywriters, you will be briefing them at some length on what you are trying to achieve. You obviously can't include all the details of your brief in your purchase order, and it shouldn't be necessary anyway. They should be making notes as you brief them. But it is useful to keep notes for your own reference, so that when you get their work back, you can recall what you asked them to do.

For example, notes of a design brief for a simple garden centre ad might be along the following lines:

- Ten-word headline
- Two illustrations – one long photograph, one line illustration
- Allow 200 words of copy; can be split into two sections of 100 words each
- Image – try to capture 'cottage garden' atmosphere, perhaps use a border of climbing plants.

What information your purchase order contains depends on the job, and on what you want to specify. But all purchase orders should state at least the following three items:

- What it is you are buying (eg design, artwork, typesetting)
- The date by which it is required
- The agreed price for the job.

A sample purchase order is shown in Fig. 29.

WHAT TO EXPECT

Most professionals will be happy to let you know exactly what they are prepared to do, and what it will cost. But it helps if you have some idea beforehand what to expect from each.

Using designers

When working with a designer, it is best to start with a telephone call to see whether they are able to do the job, followed by a full brief in the form of a personal discussion.

The brief should be as full as possible, but don't feel that you must know exactly what you want before you see them. A good designer should put forward his or her own ideas, and suggest ways of achieving what you want. The brief should therefore be a two-way process. On the other hand, don't let the designer dominate the discussion and persuade you to accept a design which looks superb but doesn't actually do anything to sell your product!

On the basis of your brief, the designer will be able to quote you a price for doing the layout – and the final artwork if the same person is doing both. You should get a written quote and/or confirm the agreed price yourself in your purchase order.

Having done the layout, the designer will present it to you for approval. You are under no obligation to accept the first version they come up with. If it genuinely doesn't conform to your brief, then you can ask them to change it, and they should do so at no extra cost. You can even reject it completely and hire another designer, but if you took care in choosing your designer in the first place, that shouldn't be necessary. If the layout conforms to your brief but doesn't look right, then the designer will change it, but might charge you extra, although that is unlikely.

If the designer is also doing your artwork, it will be presented to you for checking, and for passing on to the printer or the publication in which you are advertising. Make the following checks:

- Is everything there?

- Has the designer followed the agreed layout?

- Is the artwork clear, with no dirty marks?

- Are the pictures and text correctly aligned?

If there are any mistakes the designer should correct them free of charge. When setting the designer a deadline, make sure you allow a few days for such last-minute corrections before the artwork is due at the printers.

This check is important, because having checked the artwork, you can't hold the designer responsible for any errors that slip through.

Picture libraries

Picture libraries work in different ways. The usual procedure is for you to contact them – a telephone call is often sufficient, but a letter gives you a permanent record. Tell them what kind of picture you want, and whether you want colour or black and white. They will send you a selection, together with the prices, and you can make your choice.

You should keep any pictures you decide to use and return the rest immediately. If you decide not to use any, you simply return them all. While they are in your possession, you are responsible for them, and you are liable for any loss or damage. This can vary from about £25 for a print or duplicate transparency to hundreds of pounds for an original. They should therefore be handled with care, and always sent by registered post or delivered by hand, so that there is some proof of delivery.

The picture library usually holds the **copyright** in the photographs they send you, and you may be asked to acknowledge them when you use any. The usual form is simply '................ Picture Library' in small letters alongside the photograph.

The price of a photograph usually depends on the size at which you intend to reproduce it, and the print run of the brochure or publication.

You will usually only be paying for the *use* of the photograph, and you will be required to return it when you have finished with it. Your fee also only entitles you to use it once. Some libraries may want to charge a 'research fee' whether you use anything or not. It's best to check their terms and conditions carefully before ordering anything.

Using photographers

As with your designer, ensure that any professional photographer knows just what you want. You should first give him or her a copy of your layout, but there is certainly scope for the photographer to present ideas to you as well. Good photographers have an eye for composition, and for effects that the rest of us sometimes miss; they can often suggest different ways of approaching a particular shot.

When you have decided exactly what you want the photographer should be able to give you a quote for the job. Make sure that you are fully aware of what you are paying for. For example:

- Will you get more than one shot of each subject so that you can choose the one you like best?

- What size of prints or transparencies will you get?

- Do you want the negatives?

But if the brief is very specific and the required photograph very simple, you may find that the photographer only quotes for one picture, and that if you want extra shots, there is an extra charge.

If you want them, the photographer should also supply reference prints – small black and white prints, the precise size for the layout – so that you can paste them down on your artwork to indicate to the printer where each picture is to go. If your layout is fairly simple, reference prints aren't really necessary. Whatever you decide, make sure that the price the photographer quotes you includes everything you want.

As with the designer, you are under no obligation to accept the photographer's pictures if they clearly aren't what you asked for. However, you will have to pay the agreed price if the photograph does reasonably conform to your brief, even if you decide not to use it.

Using illustrators

Illustrators work in a very similar way to designers. Once you have found one to suit your needs, brief her or him on exactly what you want. It is especially necessary to establish the size and shape of the illustrations you need. If you want a formal record, provide a purchase order.

As with the designer and the photographer, you are under no obligation to use their illustrations if they clearly aren't what you asked for.

Using copywriters

You will work with freelance copywriters in the same way as with designers and illustrators – giving them a full brief, obtaining a price for the job, and setting a deadline.

Copywriters will often spend a couple of hours, or even more, with their clients, discussing their needs and their business – even touring the premises. They are trying to get a 'feel' for the business, so that when they sit down to write the copy, they can write from first-hand knowledge. A great deal will depend on the job, and on how thoroughly you have prepared your brief. A simple ad with a well-prepared brief will not need that kind of in-depth investigation on the part of the copywriter. You may also find copywriters coming back to you to get your approval for new ideas which may only occur to them as they write.

When the copy is done, it will be presented to you for your approval. If it obviously doesn't conform to your brief, then you can reject it, and either get the copywriter to do it again or go elsewhere. This rarely happens, however; it is more likely that a few changes will be made. Unless they are extensive, the copywriter is unlikely to try to charge extra for them.

Typesetting

If your copy is correctly marked up, your purchase order will be very simple. It will simply say 'Please set the enclosed copy as marked up, to the measure shown on the enclosed layout', and show the date it is needed and the agreed price. The typesetter will then set it in the typeface and size specified, and will provide you with a photocopy of the setting for checking.

Check the photocopy carefully against the original to ensure that it is correct. Most typesetters are extremely accurate, and some check their work before sending it out, but there will always be the odd error. Apart from spelling and punctuation mistakes, you should look out for such things as dirty marks, lines not **justified** (with straight margins on the left and the right), and lines not centred when they should be.

If you find any errors made by the typesetter, they should be marked in red, and they will be corrected free of charge. Any errors in the original copy which the typesetter has simply reproduced, or any changes you have decided on subsequently should be marked in blue. You could be charged extra for these changes, but if there are only a few minor ones the typesetter may not bother.

Working with printers

The first step in dealing with printers is to obtain a **written estimate** for the job you want done. Unlike many of the people discussed above, printers will always give you a written estimate provided they know exactly what you want.

In addition to size, the printer will need to know

- the number of colours you intend to use
- the number of photographs or transparencies
- the **weight** of paper you want.

You should discuss the paper with the printer, and ask to see examples of various weights. Weights are given in **grams per square metre** (gsm); as a general rule, the heavier the paper, the more 'up-market' the

Oakwood Furniture Ltd

45 Woodside Road · Valley Industrial Estate · Brookton

20th January 199X

James Collins Printers
17 Quay Road
Brookton

PURCHASE ORDER

Please supply:

Required:	Printing and delivery of Oakwood Furniture brochure
Size:	A4 folded twice to give final size of $\frac{1}{3}$ A4
Colour:	Four-colour on both sides
Material:	135gsm art paper
Supplied:	Artwork and five colour prints
Special instructions:	Please note the instructions in attached letter dated 20th January, and cropping and sizing instructions provided with colour prints
Delivery:	Required by 5th February 199X
Price:	£700.00 as quoted by you, 18th January 199X (Estimate No. 1234)

(*Signature*)

John Brown
Proprietor

Fig. 30. Sample purchase order for a printer.

appearance of the final brochure – and the more expensive it is! Ask to see a sample of the paper to be used.

Details of what is required in the way of artwork, illustrations and overlays are given in chapter 8. If you are sending it away, send a covering letter explaining anything which is not obvious from the artwork or overlays, together with a purchase order along the lines of that in Fig. 30. If your printer is local, then you can take the artwork and other enclosures by hand and explain in person anything you think is unclear. It is still a good idea, however, to enclose an explanatory letter so as to avoid any possible misunderstanding later.

Before doing the print run, the printer should send you a **proof** to check. If it is a colour job, you should insist on a colour proof. When you get the proof, you should check the following:

- Is everything there? It is not unheard of for a small piece of the artwork to be missing.

- Have all the colours been printed throughout the brochure?

- Are the colours right, and have the photographs been reproduced in their true colours?

- Is it in **register**? Register is the correct positioning of one colour on top of another. A piece of work is out of register, for example, if you can see a strip of yellow peeping out from the edge of a green section. That means that the cyan has not been positioned exactly on top of the yellow. The text can also be out of register, resulting in the letters looking blurred.

- Are there ink or dirty marks on it?

Depending on the size of the brochure, the proof may come in the form of one or more large sheets, with everything shown on one side. This means that it won't be in page order. Don't worry about that – the final printing and folding will put it all in the right order.

When you have checked the proof, return it to the printers with any comments and they will print and fold the brochure.

DEALING WITH DISPUTES

Overcharging
How do you know whether the price your specialist has quoted you is fair, and that you are not being overcharged or cheated? As in most

business dealings, a 'fair' price means one which the supplier is prepared to charge, and the customer prepared to pay. However, you can easily establish what the 'going rate' for the job is simply by asking other professionals to quote.

When your requirements are fairly simple to explain, as with typesetting and printing, it is always a good idea to shop around, and get about three different estimates. (You should still ask to see examples of their work, however, to ensure that the cheapest isn't also the worst quality.)

With designers and copywriters you can't do this. It's not really feasible to give a full brief to three different people in order to get three different estimates for each job. However, if you phone a few freelancers and give them an idea of what is likely to be involved, they will often be prepared to give you an indication of what they would charge. This will not be a firm quote and if you subsequently hire them, you won't be able to hold them to it, but it will help you decide whether the quote you have received is about right.

If you have defined the job fully, and agreed with your supplier exactly what you're paying for, there should be few problems with 'hidden extras'. But if you don't know what is included in the price, you could find yourself paying more than you anticipated. This doesn't necessarily mean that the person concerned is trying to cheat you. It can simply be the result of a genuine misunderstanding about what is included and what is an extra. So before you accept an estimate, make sure that you both agree what it includes, preferably in writing.

If a dispute does arise over charging, it can usually be resolved amicably; most professionals prefer this if only to protect their reputations. But very occasionally there will be a problem which wasn't foreseen and which can't be resolved so easily. Where do you stand then?

- If the supplier charges something as an extra which you think ought to have been included, then look at what was agreed on. A supplier is only obliged to provide the service specified in your agreement (whether written or verbal). A photographer would be entitled to charge extra for reference prints, for example, or a typesetter for a special typeface, if neither their estimate nor your purchase order or brief mentioned them.

- If the supplier makes an obviously unfair extra charge, such as charging to correct their own mistakes, then you should simply withhold payment, even if it is not mentioned in the agreement. You obviously can't cover every eventuality in your agreement, and if the supplier is foolish enough to pursue a claim for such a payment in the courts, you will find the law on your side.

The final product

Disputes are unlikely to arise as a result of poor quality work, because of the various checks at each stage. You will approve the designer's layout and artwork, the copywriter's copy, the photographer's or artist's illustrations, the typesetter's setting and the printer's proof, so any disagreements can be ironed out then. If you don't like something at that stage, then it is usually for one of four reasons:

- They haven't followed your instructions. They should then make the necessary changes, or redo the job, at no extra cost. If they refuse, you are entitled to reject their work, refuse to pay, and go elsewhere.

- They have followed your instructions, but have made some mistakes. They should then correct their errors at no extra charge.

- They have followed your instructions, but you don't like the results. You will have to pay the price agreed, and can negotiate an extra charge for them to make the changes you want. If you can't agree on a price for the changes you can go elsewhere, but you are still liable for the original charge.

- Your instructions weren't clear. You will probably have to pay for the job and any changes you want made. However, you could negotiate on any extra charges, as the suppliers should also have ensured that they knew what you wanted.

Disputes over brochures

One other possible source of dispute can arise with the printing of brochures. You may occasionally find that there is a problem with the final brochures, even after you have checked the proof. For example, the printer might not give the ink enough time to dry completely before folding them, which can result in smudging. If that or any similar printing problem arises, you are entitled to ask for the job to be redone at no extra charge.

If, however, you want to use the brochures immediately, and feel that they are usable despite the problem, you should be able to negotiate a reduction in the printer's price. If you aren't able to come to an amicable arrangement, consult your local Trading Standards Officer, as they could be classified as substandard goods.

CHECKLIST

- Have you some examples of the work of the specialists you are considering hiring? Are you satisfied that their style and quality are what you are looking for?

- Do you know the going rate for the job you want done?

- Have you defined the job clearly?

- Do you know exactly what is included in the price agreed?

- Does the work conform to what was agreed?

- If you are not happy with the result, can you establish who is responsible?

- Do you know how to sort out any disputes?

10
Measuring the Results

Your ad has appeared, you have had any response you are going to get, or any sales the ad is likely to generate, but how do you measure whether it has been successful or not? How many sales has it generated? Did it perform better than a different ad last year?

WHAT IS SUCCESS?

Success in advertising can be very difficult to quantify, unless you have very large sums of money for market research. You must first decide what your criteria for success are.

• Are you simply looking for a vague 'increase' in sales, or do you have a percentage increase in mind?

• Is your aim just to maintain your current market share?

• Do you need to get a certain return on your advertising expenditure simply to cover your costs and overheads? (This applies particularly to direct response ads).

• Do you see your success in comparative terms – if your current ad leads to more sales than your previous one then it is successful?

How you see success depends on your reason for advertising in the first place; no hard and fast rule can be applied to all circumstances. Once you have clarified your criteria, however, you must attempt to assess your ads, otherwise how do you know whether you are on the right track? Here are some techniques to help you.

MEASURING RESPONSE

If you have invested in a direct response ad, measuring the response is not difficult. The coupon on each ad should be coded, so that you can

Month	Ad Code	Budget	Ad Cost	Enquiries	Cost per enquiry	Sales	Cost per sale
January	HG2J		£325.80	457	£0.71	236	£1.38
	PT1J		£362.50	320	£1.13	184	£1.97
	CL2J	£1200	£450.71	621	£0.73	347	£1.30
			£1139.01	1398	£0.81	767	£1.49
February	HG1F		£334.75	503	£0.67	248	£1.35
	PT2F		£353.60	307	£1.15	159	£2.22
	BR2F	£700	£210.11	416	£0.51	218	£0.96
			£898.46	1226	£0.73	625	£1.44
March	HG2M		£325.80	393	£0.83	147	£2.22
	CL1M	£750	£461.25	582	£0.79	206	£2.24
			£787.05	975	£0.80	353	£2.23
April	PT1A		£362.50	316	£1.15	179	£2.03
	BR1A	£575	£219.20	372	£0.59	209	£1.05
			£581.70	688	£0.85	388	£1.50

Fig. 31. Measuring the response to advertising.

identify both the ad and the publication in which it appeared. A three-part code might be useful – the first part to identify the publication, the second to identify the ad, and the third to indicate when it appeared. The coupon for version 1 of an ad appearing in *Micro User* in January, for example, might be coded MU1J. When the coupons come in, you simply sort them according to their codes; you can then work out the cost per enquiry and, later, if the enquiry is translated into a sale, the cost per sale.

Cost per enquiry and cost per sale

The **cost per enquiry** is worked out by taking the *total* cost of the ad (in other words any design, photography, printing and postage costs, as well as the space cost) and dividing it by the number of enquiries received.

The **cost per sale** is worked out by dividing the total cost of the ad by the number of actual sales made.

Suppose you spent a total of £500 on a direct response ad, and got 1000 enquiries; your cost per *enquiry* would be 50p. If only 500 of those enquiries actually bought your product, the cost per *sale* would be £1. Any items which were ordered and subsequently returned should be excluded from the calculation, as they are not really sales.

In most cases it is the cost per *enquiry* which is the best measure of the ad, while the cost per sale may give you an indication of how good the follow-up is, and how popular the product. If you use the cost per sale to measure your ad's success, you could get a distorted view. It could be that the ad worked very well, but that something went wrong in converting the enquiries into sales. In that case, you shouldn't be tampering with your ads, but looking into what is wrong with the subsequent follow-up. So always use both calculations to get the full picture.

If you measure the response of each ad in a whole campaign, or a series of campaigns, you can make a number of comparisons:

- between media

- between ads

- between different times of the year.

In order to be able to make such an assessment, you need to tabulate your results along the lines shown opposite. It is vitally important to keep track of what you actually spend on your advertising, as well as what you have budgeted.

Customer feedback

Not everyone can use direct response advertising, of course. For other advertisers the measurement techniques are neither as simple nor as accurate.

One technique, used extensively by industries where the first contact is by phone (such as double glazing, loft conversion and other household improvement industries, where clients usually phone for an estimate) is to get **feedback** from the customer. The telephonist who first takes the call simply asks customers where they first heard of the company. But it can also be used when the first contact is face to face; or, indeed, the customer can be asked to fill in a questionnaire.

This enables you to measure how many of your customers responded to each of a wide variety of advertisements and media, as well as to word-of-mouth publicity. It is not quite as accurate as direct response, especially if you use a number of different ads and media, because many people will have responded to an overall image of your company derived from a number of sources, and will be unable to identify one in particular.

Market research

Research into the public's response to certain ads or images on a national scale is very expensive, and not to be recommended unless you have the money to do it properly. But if your market is local, it might be worth employing a market research organisation to conduct a survey for you (see 'Market research and analysis' in *Yellow Pages*). If they combine your survey with others they are doing, the costs will be much lower than if you ask them to carry out a survey just for you.

Market researchers canvass a cross-section of the public, either by telephone or in the street, and you would have to discuss exactly what you wanted them to find out for you. As with customer feedback, the results will not be as accurate a measure of an individual ad's success as a cost per enquiry calculation in direct response advertising.

Measuring sales

You should, in the normal course of your business, be measuring sales through the year. These sales can be related to advertising effort, as well as other factors, to try to discover its effect on the business. If, for example, Mary Davies's bookshop showed a surge in sales the first time she advertised in September, and if there were no other factors to account for the increase, then the extra turnover could be attributed to the advertisement.

It is rarely as clear-cut as that, however. The most you can usually hope for is to see the effect of a whole campaign in your sales figures, rather than being able to measure the success of individual ads.

If the purpose of your campaign was to create a particular image, then this is a good way of assessing it. Market research might tell you whether people responded positively or negatively to the campaign, but only your sales figures can tell you whether the response was positive enough to make people buy the product. You need to measure your sales over a long period, say three to six months, and compare them with the same period in previous years to see how successful your image is.

MAKING COMPARISONS

Comparing ads

When you have some idea how your ads have performed, you can begin to compare them, to see which design or format works best for you. The easiest way of doing this, of course, is simply to compare the public's response to them, using whichever of the above techniques of measurement is most applicable. The ad which got the best response is obviously the one to repeat.

It is not always so easy, however. Your particular ads might not lend themselves very easily to these techniques, or your initial aims might have been such that you can't judge success in a quantifiable way. Even when they are, you have to be careful when comparing ads that you are comparing like with like. If two different ads were used in two different publications, for example, can you be sure that the difference in response is due to the different formats and not the different media?

Critical evaluation

So whether you also make a quantitative judgement or not, you should look at all your ads critically and qualitatively, to see whether they can be improved. They may be successful, but could they be even more so? Don't repeat a particular ad just because it performed better than another one. Ask yourself why. Are there elements in it which could be improved? Look at each ad, and ask yourself the following questions:

1. Does it conform to your brief?

2. Is it well targeted?

3. Is it attention-grabbing and interesting?

4. Is it believable?

5. Is it persuasive and does it prove its case?

Comparing media

You will almost certainly get different response rates from different media, and it pays to examine each critically to try to discover why. If one publication has performed much worse than another, don't reject it out of hand. There may be a good reason. Ask yourself:

1. Are the ads different? If so, are you sure it's the medium that's at fault, not the ad?

2. Did the ads appear at different times in different publications? Could the timing have affected the response?

3. Was it only a black and white ad in the midst of a number of colour ones?

If the answer to all the questions is 'no', then it could be that you chose the wrong medium. But what could have been wrong with it?

4. Is the publication ABC certified?

5. Is it targeted at precisely the audience you wanted to reach, not only in terms of interests, but also in terms of socio-economic position?

6. Is it a free-distribution publication? The response to these is often poorer than to those that people have paid for.

7. How does the *readership* (as opposed to the *circulation*) compare with more successful media? Some publications have many more readers per copy than others, which can affect the response to advertising.

You may find that even after a comprehensive analysis you can't discover why one medium has performed better than another. It could be sheer coincidence, and another ad in the same publication later could do very well.

On the other hand, there are media which just do not produce the same response to certain types of ad as others, for no reason that the advertiser can discern. The only sure way of finding out, as with almost all aspects of advertising, is trial and error.

Comparing times of years

There is no doubt that *when* you advertise can play an important part in the success of your campaign. If all your ads at a certain time of the year did worse than you expected, it might not have been the fault of the ads or the media. It could just have been the wrong time of the year.

Look carefully at your timing in relation to your product. Is there any reason why your audience might not be interested in your product at that particular time? Were your ads geared to the time of publication? Mary Davies's bookshop ads, for example, appealed to different buying stimuli at different times of the year.

CHECKLIST

• What are the criteria for the success of your ads?

• What method of measuring response suits your business best – cost per enquiry, customer feedback, market research or sales figures?

• Can you establish why each ad succeeded or failed?

• If an ad in a particular publication hasn't worked, do you know whether the publication was wrong for you, and if so why?

• Was your timing right, and were your ads geared to the time of year at which they appeared?

Further Reading

If you want to take a closer look at any of the elements of advertising, the following books are particularly recommended.

MEDIA BUYING

The Effective Use of Advertising Media, 4th edition, Martyn P. Davis (Hutchinson 1992).

COPYWRITING

The Craft of Copywriting, 2nd edition, Alastair Crompton (Hutchinson 1987).

DESIGN

The Designer's Handbook, 2nd edition, Alastair Campbell (Little, Brown 1993).

REFERENCE

Creative Handbook, Reed Information Services.
BRAD (Emap Business Communications, Chalk Lane, Cockfosters Road, Barnet, Herts EN4 0BU, monthly).

GENERAL

For a look at advertising and how to do it, from one of the world's greatest copywriters:
Ogilvy on Advertising, David Ogilvy (Prion 1995).

Useful Addresses

The Advertising Association, Ashford House, 15 Wilton Road, London SW1V 1NJ. Tel: (0171) 828 2771. Brings together a wide variety of organisations concerned with advertising, from the Institute of Practitioners in Advertising (see below) to media owners. Their information centre is open to all.

The Advertising Standards Authority, Brook House, 2–16 Torrington Place, London WC1E 7HN. Tel: (0171) 580 5555. For information on legal requirements.

The British Association of Picture Libraries and Agencies, 13 Woodberry Crescent, London N10 1PJ. Tel: (0181) 444 7713.

The Direct Marketing Association (UK) Ltd, Haymarket House, 1 Oxendon Street, London SW1Y 4EE. Tel: (0171) 321 2525. Provides information on all aspects of direct mail.

The Institute of Practitioners in Advertising, 44 Belgrave Square, London SW1X 8QS. Tel: (0171) 245 9904. The trade association for the advertising industry.

The Outdoor Advertising Association, of Great Britain Ltd, 77 Newman Street, London W1A 1DX. Tel: (0171) 637 7703. The trade association for poster site owners.

Glossary

ABC certified A term used to indicate that a publication's circulation figure has been certified as accurate by the Audit Bureau of Circulations.

Artwork All the elements of an advertisement laid down to form a 'master' from which it can be printed.

Body copy The text of an ad, without the headline.

Bold type Heavy type, used for emphasis, like this: **bold**. Normal type is called medium.

Brief The process of giving information about the company and/or product to the people who are going to put an advertisement together.

Brochure A leaflet or catalogue which can be mailed or delivered by hand, or which can be inserted in a magazine or newspaper.

Bullet points A list of benefits, services, facilities or other points in a short, punchy style.

Camera-ready artwork The proper term for what is usually called just artwork.

Character A typesetting term for an individual letter, figure or symbol.

Conversational copy style A style which uses a conversation between two people to get its point over.

Copy All the words used to describe and sell a product.

Cost per enquiry A means of measuring the response to a direct response advertisement.

Cost per sale A means of measuring the effectiveness of a direct response advertisement and the subsequent follow-up.

Cost per thousand A calculation which enables an advertiser to compare the value of different publications by working out the cost of the space in relation to the circulation.

Cropping The process of 'cutting off' a section of an illustration which is the wrong shape.

Cross-head A subheading within the body copy of an advertisement.

Cut-out photograph A photograph with the background cut away.

Direct mail The distribution of advertising material direct to the public in their homes or offices, originally by mail, but now used to describe this operation whether the postal service is actually used or not.

Direct response advertisement An advertisement which invites customers to send off for a product. Usually includes a coupon to mail.

Em Typesetting measure; an em is a sixth of an inch.

Emotional buying trigger An appeal to an emotion or instinct in order to persuade people to buy a product.

Emotive copy style A style which appeals to the reader's emotions.

Factual copy style A style which simply gives the facts and figures about the product.

Flash A small device, often in the shape of a starburst, an oval or a lozenge, carrying a short punchy message. Often used to show prices or savings in an ad.

Fold line A line drawn on artwork to show the printer where a brochure is to be folded. Always drawn outside the printing area.

Gatefold A way of folding a brochure. It involves folding a single sheet three times, to form eight sides.

Gsm Grams per square metre – the unit of measurement of the weight of paper.

Half-tone Photograph turned into thousands of tiny dots for plate-making purposes.

Insert An advertising brochure which is inserted loose into a newspaper or magazine.

Italic type A sloping type, used for emphasis, like this: *italic*. Non-italic type is called roman.

Justified type Type which has a straight margin on the right as well as the left.

Keyline A line drawn on artwork to indicate a division between one colour and another.

Key words Words which attract the reader's interest, such as free, now, introducing, magic, unique, sale, etc.

Layout An accurate representation of what a finished advertisement will look like, but without the actual text or illustration.

Leading Extra space between lines of type.

Logo An emblem or device by which a product or company can be easily recognised.

Measure The length of a line of type, usually expressed in **ems**.

Media The means of putting across a message. In advertising, it includes the press, mailing lists and poster sites.

Media buying Buying or hiring the means of advertising.

Media pack A pack sent to potential advertisers by a publication. It usually consists of a rate card, a readership profile and a sample copy of the publication.

Narrative copy style A style which uses a story to illustrate the benefits of a product.

Overlaid illustrations Illustrations which overlap.

Point The unit of measurement of the height of type. There are 72 points to the inch, and 12 points to the **em**.

Press advertising Any advertising which appears in newspapers or magazines. Includes direct response advertisements, inserts, classified and display advertising.

Rate card A list of advertising rates provided by a publication.

Reference prints Black and white photographic prints which are exactly the right size and shape for an advertisement. Can be pasted down on artwork.

Roll-fold A way of folding a brochure. It involves folding a single sheet twice, to form six sides.

Rule Used in typesetting and design to denote a straight line.

Run-of-paper advertisement An advertisement which the editor of a publication can put where he likes.

Sales letter A piece of advertising in the form of a letter, usually personalised and mailed to a named individual.

Single column centimetre (scc) The usual unit of measurement of advertising space – one column wide and one centimetre deep.

Sizing Calculating and indicating what percentage reduction or enlargement is necessary for an illustration to fit the space provided on the artwork.

Solus advertisement The only advertisement on a particular page.

Space An advertising 'slot' in a newspaper or magazine.

Target audience The specific readership at which an advertisement is aimed.

Testimonial The endorsement of a product or company by someone unconnected with it.

Tint chart A chart which shows all the tints available using the four basic colours, and how to specify each.

Trim lines Lines drawn on artwork to show the printer where a brochure is to be trimmed or cut. Always drawn outside the printing area.

Typeface A particular design of lettering.

USP Unique selling proposition – a benefit which makes a particular product unique.

VFD Verified Free Distribution – a term used to indicate that a free-distribution publication's figures for the number of copies distributed have been verified.

Voluntary codes Codes of practice which the advertising industry imposes on itself. They are not voluntary in the sense that you can choose whether to obey them or not. No advertisement which breaks one of the codes will be accepted for publication.

Index